Biology
Study Guide

D1536220

HOLT, RINEHART AND WINSTON

A Harcourt Education Company

Orlando • **Austin** • New York • San Diego • Toronto • London

Printed in the United States of America

ISBN 978-0-03-069982-5   ISBN 0-03-069982-7

15 16 17 18 19   0982 14 13 12 11

4500285395

Contents

Introduction to Body Structure

Circulatory and Respiratory Systems

Digestive and Excretory Systems

The Body's Defenses

Nervous System

Hormones and the Endocrine System

Reproduction and Development

Vocabulary Review

In the space provided, explain how the terms in each pair differ in meaning.

1. cell, metabolism

_____

_____

2. heredity, mutation

_____

_____

3. natural selection, evolution

_____

_____

4. hypothesis, prediction

_____

_____

5. independent variable, dependent variable

_____

_____

6. theory, observation

_____

_____

7. cystic fibrosis, gene

_____

_____

In the space provided, write the letter of the description that best matches the term or phrase.

_____ **8.** biology

_____ **9.** control group

_____ **10.** homeostasis

_____ **11.** species

_____ **12.** reproduction

_____ **13.** ecology

_____ **14.** experiment

_____ **15.** HIV

_____ **16.** cancer

_____ **17.** pH

a. a group of organisms that are genetically similar and can produce fertile offspring

b. state of constant internal conditions

c. the study of living things

d. receives no experimental treatment

e. organisms make more of their own kind

f. the study of the interactions of living organisms

g. planned procedure to test a hypothesis

h. relative measure of the hydrogen ion concentration within a solution

i. virus that causes AIDS

j. a breakdown of the mechanism that controls cell division

Name _____ Class _____ Date _____

Test Prep Pretest

In the space provided, write the letter of the term or phrase that best completes each statement or best answers each question.

_____ 1. Biologists have found ways to use leftover potato particles
    a. to build huts.
    b. to feed tigers.
    c. to make concrete.
    d. to fuel power plants.

_____ 2. Control and experimental groups are identical except for the
    a. dependent variable.
    b. group size.
    c. independent variable.
    d. conclusions.

_____ 3. A collection of related hypotheses that have been tested many times is called a(n)
    a. prediction.
    b. observation.
    c. theory.
    d. insight.

_____ 4. What properties do all living things exhibit?
    a. cellular organization, metabolism, homeostasis, reproduction, and heredity
    b. multicellular organization, metabolism, homeostasis, reproduction, and heredity
    c. photosynthesis, metabolism, homeostasis, reproduction, and heredity
    d. cellular organization, photosynthesis, homeostasis, reproduction, and heredity

_____ 5. Almost all lung cancers can be prevented by
    a. changing your diet.
    b. eliminating the use of tobacco.
    c. staying out of the sun.
    d. exercising regularly.

In the space provided, write the letter of the description that best matches the term or phrase.

_____ 6. scientific processes

_____ 7. homeostasis

_____ 8. pH level

_____ 9. gene therapy

_____ 10. hypothesis

a. independent variable in John Harte's experiment

b. collecting observations, asking questions, forming hypotheses and making predictions, confirming predictions, and drawing conclusions.

c. an explanation that might be true

d. living things maintain relatively stable internal conditions

e. replacing a defective gene with a normal gene

Test Prep Pretest *continued*

Complete each statement by writing the correct term or phrase in the space provided.

11. A scientist collects data to test a(n) _____ .

12. All living things pass on genetic information from parent to offspring through

    a process known as _____ .

13. The change in a species' inherited traits over time is called _____ .

14. The _____ _____ _____

    has succeeded in sequencing all human chromosomes.

15. The basic unit of all organisms that can carry out all life processes is the

    _____ .

Read each question, and write your answer in the space provided.

16. Explain what role DNA plays in an organism.

    _____

    _____

    _____

17. Give an example of how a gene mutation can be beneficial.

    _____

    _____

    _____

18. Why is reproduction an essential part of living?

    _____

    _____

19. Define the first stage of a scientific investigation-observation.

    _____

    _____

    _____

20. Harte's research supported his hypothesis that acid in melting snow killed
    salamanders. Why is this hypothesis not yet accepted as a theory?

    _____

    _____

    _____

Test Prep Pretest *continued*

21. Describe interdependence in a biological community.

_____

_____

_____

22. What is the role of metabolism in life?

_____

_____

_____

_____

_____

23. Briefly describe how scientific research has contributed to the efforts to increase world food production.

_____

_____

_____

_____

24. Briefly describe recent scientific advances in finding a vaccine for HIV.

_____

_____

_____

_____

25. If the results of an experiment do not support the hypothesis that the experiment was designed to test, was the experiment a waste of time? Explain.

_____

_____

_____

_____

Skills Worksheet

Vocabulary Review

In the space provided, write the letter of the description that best matches the term or phrase.

_____ **1.** ion

_____ **2.** atom

_____ **3.** compound

_____ **4.** amino acids

_____ **5.** covalent bond

_____ **6.** ionic bond

_____ **7.** element

_____ **8.** solution

a. smallest unit of matter that cannot be broken down by chemical means

b. a substance made of the joined atoms of two or more different elements

c. atom or molecule that has lost or gained one or more electrons

d. a substance made of only one type of atom

e. one substance evenly distributed in another

f. chemical bond in which electrons are shared

g. building blocks of protein

h. attraction between oppositely charged ions

Complete each statement by writing the correct term or phrase in the space provided.

9. A(n) _____ is a substance on which an enzyme acts during a chemical reaction.

10. An organic compound with a ratio of one carbon atom to two hydrogen atoms to one oxygen atom is a(n) _____ .

11. Glucose is a(n) _____ that is a major source of energy in cells.

12. A(n) _____ is an organic compound that is not soluble in water.

13. A(n) _____ is a long chain of amino acids.

14. Subunits of DNA and RNA are called _____ .

15. DNA is a(n) _____ _____ that encodes protein sequences.

| Vocabulary Review *continued*

In the space provided, explain how the terms in each pair differ in meaning.

16. acid, base

_____

_____

_____

17. cohesion, adhesion

_____

_____

_____

18. enzyme, active site

_____

_____

_____

19. energy, activation energy

_____

_____

_____

20. DNA, RNA

_____

_____

_____

21. ATP, carbohydrate

_____

_____

_____

Skills Worksheet

Test Prep Pretest

In the space provided, write the letter of the term or phrase that best completes each statement or best answers each question.

_____ 1. Acids and bases differ in that
  a. bases dissolved in water form more hydrogen ions than do acids dissolved in water.
  b. acids dissolved in water form more hydrogen ions than do bases dissolved in water.
  c. acids dissolved in water form more hydroxide ions than do bases dissolved in water.
  d. bases have a lower pH than do acids.

_____ 2. Which of the following groups of terms is associated with carbohydrates?
  a. monosaccharide, glycogen, cellulose
  b. monosaccharide, cellulose, lipid
  c. disaccharide, polysaccharide, steroid
  d. polysaccharide, amino acid, collagen

_____ 3. The speed of a chemical reaction is increased by
  a. an enzyme.   **c.** glucose.
  b. the reactant.   **d.** ATP.

_____ 4. Which of the following enzymes helps break down starch into glucose?
  a. pepsin   **c.** catalase
  b. trypsin   **d.** amylase

_____ 5. Which of the following is not a property of water?
  a. cohesion
  b. polarity
  c. nonpolarity
  d. stores heat well

In the space provided, write the letter of the description that best matches the term or phrase.

_____ 6. atom

_____ 7. element

_____ 8. compound

_____ 9. molecule

_____ 10. electron

  a. a substance made when atoms of two or more different elements join together
  b. negatively charged atomic particle
  c. the smallest unit of matter that cannot be broken down by chemical means
  d. a group of atoms held together by covalent bonds
  e. a substance made of only one kind of atom

Complete each statement by writing the correct term or phrase in the space provided.

11. Molecules that are _____ dissolve best in water, while _____ molecules do not dissolve well in water.

12. The weak chemical attraction between water molecules are _____ bonds, while the stronger chemical bonds between the atoms of each water molecule are _____ bonds.

13. An atom or a molecule that has gained or lost one or more electrons is called a(n) _____ .

14. On the pH scale, vinegar is a(n) _____ and ammonia is a(n) _____ .

15. Two _____ that store energy are starch, which is produced by plants, and glycogen, which is produced by animals.

16. DNA and RNA, which are two kinds of _____ _____ , are made of long chains of nucleotides.

17. When sodium chloride is dissolved in water, a chemical reaction occurs in which _____ _____ is the reactant, and sodium ions and chloride ions are the _____ .

18. Enzymes are a type of _____ , which reduces the activation energy of a chemical reaction.

19. A substrate attaches to the _____ _____ of an enzyme.

20. Temperature and _____ can affect enzyme activity.

Test Prep Pretest *continued*

Questions 21–23 refer to the figures below.

A   B   C

21. Identify the class of organic compound represented by each of the molecules shown above.

_____

_____

22. For each type of compound shown above, explain the role it plays in your body.

_____

_____

_____

_____

_____

23. How can you tell whether a compound is organic or not?

_____

_____

_____

_____

Test Prep Pretest *continued*

24. Explain why living things need energy and where they get it.

_____

_____

_____

_____

_____

_____

25. Briefly describe the function of ATP in cells.

_____

_____

_____

_____

Name _____ Class _____ Date _____

Vocabulary Review

In the blanks provided, fill in the letters of the term or phrase being described.

1. uses light to produce a magnified image
   _ _ _ _ **T** _ **M** _ _ _ _ _ _ _ _ _

2. uses electrons to form a magnified image
   _ _ _ **C** _ _ _ _ **M** _ _ _ _ _ _ _ _

3. when an image appears larger
   _ _ **G** _ _ _ _ _ _ _ _ _ _

4. measure of clarity of image
   R _ _ _ _ _ _ _ _ _

5. produces three-dimensional images of living organisms
   _ _ _ _ _ **N** _ _ _ _ _ **N** _ _ _ _ _ _
   I _ _ _ _ _ _ _ _ _ _

6. all living things are made of cells
   _ _ _ **L** _ **H** _ _ _ _

7. regulates what enters and leaves a cell
   _ _ _ **L** _ _ **M** _ _ _ _ _

8. structure on which proteins are made
   _ _ **B** _ _ _ _ _

9. single-celled organism that lacks a nucleus
   _ _ _ **K** _ _ _ _ _ _

10. protrude from cell's surface and enable movement
    F _ _ _ _ _ _ _

11. carries out specific activities
    _ _ **G** _ _ _ _ _ _

12. hairlike structures
    C _ _ _ _

13. organism whose cells each have a nucleus
    _ **U** _ _ _ _ _ _ _

14. houses the cell's DNA
    _ _ **C** _ _ _ _

15. interior of cell
    _ _ _ _ **P** _ _ _ _

16. keeps cell membrane from collapsing
    _ _ _ _ **S** _ _ _ _ _ _ _

17. has a polar "head" and nonpolar "tails"
    _ _ _ **S** _ _ _ _ _ _ _

18. double layer of phospholipids
    _ _ _ _ **D** _ _ _ **L** _ _ _ _

Vocabulary Review *continued*

Complete each statement by writing the correct term or phrase in the space provided.

19. The _____ _____ is an extensive system of internal membranes that move proteins and other substances through the cell.

20. A(n) _____ is a small, membrane-bound sac.

21. The _____ _____ is the packaging and distribution center of the cell.

22. The organelles that contain the cell's digestive enzymes are

    _____ .

23. The organelles that transfer energy from organic compounds to ATP

    are _____ .

24. Organelles that use light energy to make carbohydrates from carbon dioxide

    and water are _____ .

25. The _____ _____ stores water and may contain many substances, such as ions, nutrients, and wastes.

26. The cell membrane of a plant is surrounded by a thick

    _____ _____ , which supports and protects the cell.

Name _____ Class _____ Date _____

Test Prep Pretest

In the space provided, write the letter of the term or phrase that best completes each statement or best answers each question.

_____ 1. The surface area-to-volume ratio of a small cell is
   a. greater than that of a larger cell.
   b. less than that of a larger cell.
   c. equal to that of a larger cell.
   d. not affected by the cell's size.

_____ 2. In the metric system, a micrometer (μm) is equal to 0.000001 (one millionth) of a
   a. kilometer (km).   **c.** centimeter (cm).
   b. meter (m).   **d.** millimeter (mm).

_____ 3. A protein on the cell membrane that recognizes and binds to specific substances is called a(n)
   a. marker protein.   **c.** enzyme.
   b. receptor protein.   **d.** transport protein.

_____ 4. In a eukaryotic cell, mitochondria
   a. transport materials.   **c.** produce ATP.
   b. make proteins.   **d.** control cell division.

Questions 5 and 6 refer to the figure at right.

_____ 5. The organism in the figure at right is a(n)
   a. prokaryotic cell.
   b. eukaryotic cell.
   c. plant cell.
   d. Both (b) and (c)

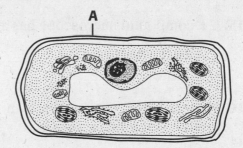

_____ 6. The structure labeled *A*
   a. supports the cell.
   b. protects the cell.
   c. surrounds the cell membrane.
   d. All of the above

Complete each statement by writing the correct term or phrase in the space provided.

7. A cell's boundary is called the _____

_____ .

8. In a bacterium, the _____ _____ provides structure and support.

9. In the cell membrane, _____ _____ aid the movement of substances into and out of a cell.

10. In plant cells, rigidity is provided by a large, membrane-bound sac called

the _____ _____ .

11. Nuclear _____ allow certain substances to pass into and out of the nucleus of a cell.

12. Vesicles that contain a cell's digestive enzymes are called

_____ .

13. The "head" of a phospholipid is _____ , so it is attracted

to water, while the "tails" are _____ , so they are repelled by water.

14. The cytoskeleton is a network of protein fibers that support the shape of a

cell and may be involved in the movement of _____ .

15. If a compound microscope has a $50\times$ objective lens and a $10\times$ ocular lens,

a viewed image appears _____ times larger than its actual size.

16. Mitochondria contain their own _____ , so they can produce their own proteins.

Name _____ Class _____ Date _____

Questions 17–23 refer to the figure below.

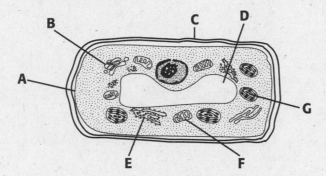

17. The structure labeled *A* is the _____ _____ .

18. The organelle labeled *B* is the _____ _____ .

19. The structure labeled *C* is the _____ _____ .

20. The structure labeled *D* is the _____ _____ .

21. The organelle labeled *E* is the _____ _____ .

22. The organelle labeled *F* is a(n) _____ .

23. The organelle labeled *G* is a(n) _____ .

Read each question, and write your answer in the space provided.

24. List the three parts of the cell theory.

_____

_____

_____

25. List the primary differences between prokaryotic cells and eukaryotic cells.

_____

_____

_____

_____

_____

Name _____ Class _____ Date _____

Vocabulary Review

In the space provided, write the letter of the description that best matches the term or phrase.

_____ 1. passive transport

_____ 2. concentration gradient

_____ 3. equilibrium

_____ 4. diffusion

_____ 5. osmosis

_____ 6. hypertonic solution

_____ 7. hypotonic solution

_____ 8. isotonic solution

_____ 9. ion channel

_____ 10. carrier protein

_____ 11. facilitated diffusion

_____ 12. active transport

_____ 13. sodium-potassium pump

_____ 14. endocytosis

_____ 15. exocytosis

_____ 16. receptor protein

_____ 17. second messenger

a. movement of a substance down the substance's concentration gradient

b. causes a cell to shrink because of osmosis

c. movement of a substance by a vesicle to the outside of a cell

d. carrier protein used in active transport

e. protein used to transport specific substances

f. transport protein through which ions can pass

g. movement of a substance by a vesicle to the inside of a cell

h. does not require energy from the cell

i. concentration of a substance is equal throughout a space

j. difference in the concentration of a substance across a space

k. diffusion of water through a selectively permeable membrane

l. causes a cell to swell because of osmosis

m. passive transport using carrier proteins

n. produces no change in cell volume because of osmosis

o. movement of a substance against the substance's concentration gradient

p. acts as a signal molecule in the cytoplasm

q. binds to a signal molecule, enabling the cell to respond to the signal molecule

Name _____ Class _____ Date _____

Test Prep Pretest

In the space provided, write the letter of the term or phrase that best completes each statement or best answers each question.

_____ 1. When a receptor protein in a cell membrane acts as an enzyme, the receptor protein
   a. changes its shape to allow the signal molecule to enter the cell.
   b. causes chemical changes in the cell.
   c. activates a second messenger that acts as a signal molecule within the cell.
   d. changes the permeability of the cell membrane.

_____ 2. Which of the following is NOT a characteristic of an ion channel?
   a. It extends from one side of the cell membrane to the other.
   b. It may or may not have a gate.
   c. It is polar, so charged substances, such as ions, can pass through the nonpolar lipid bilayer.
   d. It allows ions to move against their concentration gradient.

_____ 3. When a cell uses energy to transport a particle through the cell membrane to an area of higher concentration, the cell is using
   a. diffusion.   **c.** osmosis.
   b. active transport.   **d.** facilitated diffusion.

_____ 4. The excretion of materials to the outside of a cell by discharging them from vesicles is called
   a. exocytosis.   **c.** osmosis.
   b. endocytosis.   **d.** diffusion.

_____ 5. The mechanism that prevents sodium ions from building up inside the cell is called
   a. the sodium-potassium pump.   **c.** diffusion.
   b. endocytosis.   **d.** exocytosis.

Complete each statement by writing the correct term or phrase in the space provided.

Question 6 refers to the figure at right.

6. The process shown in the figure

   is _____ .

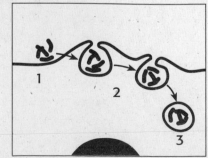

Test Prep Pretest *continued*

7. Cell-surface proteins allow a cell to _____ with other cells.

8. The _____ _____

_____ requires energy to function.

9. When a substance moves from an area of low concentration to an area of

higher concentration, the substance moves _____ its concentration gradient.

10. The movement of particles down their concentration gradient through carrier

proteins is known as _____ _____ .

11. A(n) _____ _____ amplifies the communication from a signal molecule.

12. A(n) _____ _____

_____ in the cell membrane may be opened or closed.

Questions 13–15 refer to the figures below.

A   B   C

13. Figure *A* illustrates a cell in a(n) _____ solution.

14. Figure *B* illustrates a cell in a(n) _____ solution.

15. Figure *C* illustrates a cell in a(n) _____ solution.

Read each question, and write your answer in the space provided.

16. Describe the electrical charge inside and outside a typical cell. Then explain how this affects an ion's ability to move into the cell.

_____

_____

_____

_____

17. Suppose you want to explain a concentration gradient to someone. Create a scenario that illustrates passive transport down the concentration gradient.

_____

_____

_____

_____

_____

18. Using your understanding of osmosis, describe why putting salt on a pork chop before cooking it on a grill is likely to result in a dry, tough piece of meat.

_____

_____

_____

_____

_____

19. How is facilitated diffusion different from the other passive transport processes?

_____

_____

_____

20. How does a cell consume a food particle that is too large to pass through a protein channel?

_____

_____

_____

Name _____ Class _____ Date _____

Vocabulary Review

Write the correct term from the list below in the space next to its definition.

aerobic	cellular respiration	heterotrophs
anaerobic	chlorophyll	Krebs cycle
autotrophs	electron transport chain	photosynthesis
Calvin cycle	fermentation	pigment
carbon dioxide fixation	glycolysis	thylakoids
carotenoids		

_____ **1.** the process by which light energy is converted to chemical energy

_____ **2.** organisms that use energy from sunlight or inorganic substances to make organic compounds

_____ **3.** organisms that get energy by consuming food

_____ **4.** the process by which cells harvest energy from food

_____ **5.** a substance that absorbs light

_____ **6.** the primary pigment involved in photosynthesis

_____ **7.** absorb wavelengths of light different from those absorbed by chlorophyll

_____ **8.** the series of molecules down which excited electrons are passed in a thylakoid membrane

_____ **9.** the transfer of carbon dioxide to organic compounds

_____ **10.** a series of enzyme-assisted chemical reactions that produces a three-carbon sugar molecule

_____ **11.** a process that requires oxygen

_____ **12.** a process that does not require oxygen

_____ **13.** the process by which glucose is broken down to pyruvate

_____ **14.** a series of enzyme-assisted chemical reactions following glycolysis that produces carbon dioxide

_____ **15.** the recycling of NAD^+ under anaerobic conditions

_____ **16.** disk-shaped structures inside chloroplasts

Skills Worksheet

Test Prep Pretest

In the space provided, write the letter of the term or phrase that best completes each statement or best answers each question.

_____ **1.** Photosynthetic organisms get energy from
  a. inorganic substances.   **c.** autotrophs.
  b. light.   **d.** heterotrophs.

_____ **2.** Which of the following correctly sequences the flow of energy?
  a. bacteria, fungus, rabbit   **c.** sun, grass, rabbit, fox
  b. bacteria, sun, flower, deer   **d.** sun, hawk, mouse

_____ **3.** ATP molecules
  a. produce NADPH.
  b. contain five phosphate groups.
  c. can both store energy and provide it for metabolic reactions.
  d. help a plant produce carbon dioxide.

_____ **4.** In glycolysis,
  a. aerobic processes occur.
  b. four ATP molecules are produced.
  c. four ADP molecules are produced.
  d. glucose is produced.

_____ **5.** Which of the following environmental factors does NOT directly influence the rate of photosynthesis?
  a. light intensity   **c.** carbon dioxide concentration
  b. oxygen concentration   **d.** temperature

_____ **6.** Carbon dioxide fixation in the Calvin cycle requires
  a. ATP and NADPH.   **c.** ADP and NADPH.
  b. ATP and NADP$^+$.   **d.** ATP and oxygen.

_____ **7.** When this gas is available, aerobic respiration follows glycolysis.
  a. carbon dioxide   **c.** hydrogen
  b. oxygen   **d.** water vapor

Question 8 refers to the chemical equation below.

$$3CO_2 + 3H_2O \xrightarrow{\text{light}} C_3H_6O_3 + 3O_2$$

_____ **8.** This equation summarizes the overall process of
  a. cellular respiration.   **c.** the Calvin cycle.
  b. photosynthesis.   **d.** the Krebs cycle.

_____ **9.** Which of the following is NOT part of cellular respiration?
        a. electron transport chain   **c.** Krebs cycle
        b. glycolysis   **d.** Calvin cycle

_____**10.** Electrons in pigment molecules become excited
        a. when light strikes a thylakoid.
        b. when water molecules are broken down.
        c. during light-independent reactions.
        d. during the Calvin cycle.

Complete each statement by writing the correct term or phrase in the space provided.

11. The carrier protein that transports hydrogen ions across thylakoid membranes and produce ATP acts as both a(n) _____

_____ and a(n) _____ .

12. The _____ _____ is the most common method of carbon dioxide fixation.

13. Aerobic respiration occurs in the _____ of eukaryotic cells.

14. Plants use sugars produced during _____ to make organic compounds.

15. During photosynthesis, light energy is converted to _____ energy.

16. During anaerobic processes, NADH transfers electrons to the pyruvate produced during _____ .

17. Glycolysis is a biochemical pathway that breaks down a six-carbon glucose molecule to two three-carbon _____ .

18. During aerobic respiration, pyruvate is first converted to acetyl-CoA, which enters the _____ _____ .

19. During cellular respiration, a cell produces most of its energy through _____ respiration.

20. Light-absorbing _____ are located in the membranes of

    _____ .

Read each question, and write your answer in the space provided.

21. Explain how the metabolism of heterotrophs differs from that of autotrophs.

    _____

    _____

    _____

    _____

    _____

    _____

22. Explain how ATP provides energy for cells.

    _____

    _____

    _____

23. Briefly explain how ATP is produced by electron transport chains during
    photosynthesis.

    _____

    _____

    _____

    _____

    _____

    _____

    _____

    _____

    _____

    _____

Test Prep Pretest *continued*

24. Describe how environmental factors affect the rate of photosynthesis.

_____

_____

_____

_____

_____

25. Explain the benefits and uses of lactic acid fermentation and alcoholic fermentation.

_____

_____

_____

_____

_____

Name _____ Class _____ Date _____

Vocabulary Review

In the space provided, write the letter of the term or phrase that best completes each statement or best answers each question.

_____ 1. An organism's reproductive cells, such as sperm or egg cells, are called
    a. genes.
    c. gametes.
    b. chromosomes.
    d. zygotes.

_____ 2. A form of asexual reproduction in bacteria is
    a. binary fission.
    c. mitosis.
    b. trisomy.
    d. development.

_____ 3. A segment of DNA that codes for a protein or RNA molecule is a
    a. chromosome.
    c. chromatid.
    b. gene.
    d. centromere.

_____ 4. At the beginning of cell division, DNA and the proteins associated with the DNA coil into a structure called a(n)
    a. chromatid.
    c. centromere.
    b. autosome.
    d. chromosome.

_____ 5. The two exact copies of DNA that make up each chromosome are called
    a. homologous chromosomes.
    c. chromatids.
    b. centromeres.
    d. autosomes.

_____ 6. The two chromatids of a chromosome are attached at a point called the
    a. diploid.
    c. spindle.
    b. centriole.
    d. centromere.

_____ 7. Chromosomes that are similar in size, shape, and genetic content are called which of the following?
    a. homologous chromosomes
    c. diploid
    b. haploid
    d. karyotypes

_____ 8. When a cell contains two sets of chromosomes, it is said to be
    a. haploid.
    c. diploid.
    b. binary.
    d. saturated.

_____ 9. When a cell contains one set of chromosomes, it is said to be
    a. haploid.
    c. diploid.
    b. separated.
    d. homologous.

_____ 10. The fertilized egg, the first cell of a new individual, is called a(n)
    a. autosome.
    c. organism.
    b. zygote.
    d. chromosome.

Vocabulary Review *continued*

_____**11.** A photo of the chromosomes in a dividing cell, arranged by size, is a(n)
  a. electronic scan.   **c.** X ray.
  b. karyotype.   **d.** anaphase.

_____**12.** What are chromosomes not directly involved in determining the sex of an individual?
  a. asexual chromosomes   **c.** autosomes
  b. chromatids   **d.** haploid

_____**13.** Chromosomes that contain genes that will determine the sex of the individual are called
  a. X chromosomes.   **c.** Y chromosomes.
  b. sex chromosomes.   **d.** autosomes.

_____**14.** The repeated sequence of growth and division during the life of a cell is called the
  a. cell cycle.   **c.** binary fission.
  b. cytokinesis.   **d.** amniocentesis.

_____**15.** The first three phases of the cell cycle are called
  a. anaphase.   **c.** mitosis.
  b. interphase.   **d.** synthesis phase.

_____**16.** What is the process during which the nucleus of a cell is divided into two nuclei?
  a. fertilization   **c.** mitosis
  b. disjunction   **d.** cytokinesis

_____**17.** The process during cell division in which the cytoplasm divides is called
  a. cytokinesis.   **c.** interphase.
  b. trisomy.   **d.** mitosis.

_____**18.** What is the uncontrolled division of cells?
  a. Down syndrome   **c.** cancer
  b. mutation   **d.** trisomy

_____**19.** Cell structures made of individual microtubule fibers that are involved in moving chromosomes during cell division are called
  a. chromatids.   **c.** centrioles.
  b. fertilizers.   **d.** spindles.

Skills Worksheet

Test Prep Pretest

In the space provided, write the letter of the term or phrase that best completes each statement or best answers each question.

_____ 1. As a cell prepares to divide, a DNA molecule and its associated proteins coil to form a
  a. chromatid.
  b. gene.
  c. chromosome.
  d. centromere.

_____ 2. What is the number of chromosomes found in a human body cell?
  a. 23   **c.** 48
  b. 46   **d.** 64

_____ 3. The sex of a human offspring is determined by
  a. the female.
  b. the male.
  c. both the female and the male.
  d. neither the female nor the male.

_____ 4. Bacteria reproduce through an asexual process called
  a. meiosis.
  b. cytokinesis.
  c. interphase.
  d. binary fission.

_____ 5. In plant cells, cytokinesis requires the formation of a new
  a. Golgi apparatus.
  b. cell wall.
  c. centromere.
  d. series of protein threads.

_____ 6. Gene mutations that result in cancer often cause the
  a. overproduction of growth-promoting proteins.
  b. underproduction of growth-promoting proteins.
  c. activation of control proteins that slow or stop the cell cycle.
  d. Both (a) and (c)

_____ 7. Which of the following is NOT part of the spindle apparatus in animal cells?
  a. microtubules   **c.** spindle fibers
  b. belt of protein threads   **d.** centrioles

Complete each statement by writing the correct term or phrase in the space provided.

8. A(n) _____ is a segment of DNA that transmits informa-

tion from parent to offspring.

9. An individual with an extra copy of chromosome 21 demonstrates traits

collectively known as _____ _____ .

10. The 22 pairs of chromosomes in human somatic cells that are the same in

males and females are called _____ .

11. The human chromosomes that determine an individual's sex are called the

_____ _____ .

Questions 12–17 refer to the sequence below.

$$G_1 \longrightarrow S \longrightarrow G_2 \longrightarrow M \longrightarrow C$$

12. The sequence above represents the _____

_____ .

13. The S in the sequence represents the phase in which

_____ _____ occurs.

14. Phases G_1, S, and G_2 in the sequence above are collectively called

_____ .

15. Each individual protein structure that helps to move the chromosomes apart

during mitosis is called a(n) _____ .

16. A disease caused by uncontrolled cell division is _____ .

17. In the first stage of binary fission, the DNA is _____ .

Read each question, and write your answer in the space provided.

18. What happens to the structure of DNA in your cells prior to cell division?

_____

_____

_____

Test Prep Pretest *continued*

19. Explain the difference in the number of chromosomes between a frog somatic cell and a frog egg cell.

_____

_____

_____

20. What happens when nondisjunction takes place during cell division?

_____

_____

_____

_____

21. Describe what happens at each checkpoint during the cell cycle.

_____

_____

_____

_____

_____

22. What are the four stages of mitosis in the correct order?

_____

_____

23. Explain the events that take place during each stage of mitosis.

_____

_____

_____

_____

_____

_____

_____

24. Describe the events that take place during each phase of interphase.

_____

_____

_____

_____

_____

_____

_____

25. List four types of events that take place in a eukaryotic organism, such as a deer, that require cell division.

_____

_____

_____

_____

Name _____ Class _____ Date _____

Vocabulary Review

Complete the crossword puzzle using the clues provided.

ACROSS

6. gamete-producing process that occurs in male reproductive organs

7. the kind of reproduction in which two parents form haploid cells that join to produce offspring

9. female gamete

11. occurs during prophase I of meiosis

12. a haploid plant reproductive cell produced by meiosis

13. form of cell division that halves the number of chromosomes

14. the type of assortment that involves the random distribution of homologous chromosomes during meiosis

DOWN

1. the haploid phase of a plant that produces gametes by mitosis

2. the process in most animals that produces diploid zygotes

3. an individual produced by asexual reproduction

4. the kind of reproduction in which a single parent passes copies of all its genes to its offspring

5. the name for the cycle that spans from one generation to the next

7. male gametes

8. diploid phase of a plant that produces spores

10. occurs in the ovaries

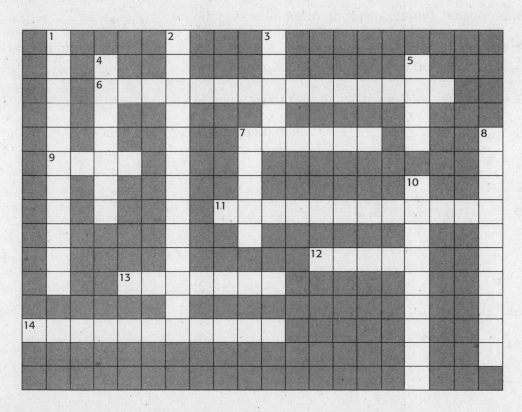

Skills Worksheet

Test Prep Pretest

Complete each statement by writing the correct term or phrase in the space provided.

1. Asexual reproduction limits _____ diversity.

2. Spermatogenesis produces _____ sperm cells.

3. Asexual reproduction methods include _____ ,

   fragmentation, and _____ .

4. In the haploid life cycle, gametes are produced by _____ ,

   and the zygote is produced by _____ .

5. When corresponding portions of chromatids on two homologous

   chromosomes change places, _____-_____
   has occurred.

6. Only one ovum is produced by _____ .

7. In plants that have alternation of generations, the haploid

   _____ produces the gametes.

8. Increased genetic variation often increases the rate of _____ .

9. Meiosis in plants often produces _____ , haploid cells
   that later lead to the production of gametes.

10. Crossing-over is an efficient way to produce _____

    _____ , which increases genetic diversity.

Test Prep Pretest *continued*

Questions 11–14 refer to the figure below.

A   B   C

11. The process shown above is called _____ .

12. In the process shown above, label *A* refers to _____ .

13. In the process shown above, label *B* refers to _____

and _____ .

14. In the process shown above, label *C* refers to _____ .

Read each question, and write your answer in the space provided.

15. Describe the similarities and differences between the formation of male and female gametes.

_____

_____

_____

_____

_____

16. Identify and describe the three types of asexual reproduction.

_____

_____

_____

_____

Test Prep Pretest *continued*

17. What is the difference between anaphase I and anaphase II?
Why is the difference significant?

_____

_____

_____

_____

_____

_____

18. Describe the haploid and diploid life cycles.

_____

_____

_____

_____

_____

_____

19. Describe the advantages and disadvantages of sexual reproduction.

_____

_____

_____

_____

_____

20. How does crossing-over affect evolution?

_____

_____

_____

_____

_____

Vocabulary Review

In the space provided, write the letter of the description that best matches the term or phrase.

_____ 1. heredity

_____ 2. genetics

_____ 3. monohybrid cross

_____ 4. true-breeding

_____ 5. P generation

_____ 6. F_1 generation

_____ 7. F_2 generation

_____ 8. alleles

_____ 9. dominant

_____ 10. recessive

_____ 11. homozygous

_____ 12. heterozygous

_____ 13. genotype

_____ 14. phenotype

_____ 15. law of segregation

_____ 16. law of independent assortment

a. the alleles of a particular gene are different

b. the two alleles for a trait separate when gametes are formed

c. the alleles of different genes separate independently of one another during gamete formation

d. not expressed when the dominant form of the trait is present

e. passing of traits from parents to offspring

f. all the offspring display only one form of a particular trait

g. the expressed form of a trait

h. first two individuals crossed in a breeding experiment

i. physical appearance of a trait

j. a cross that considers one pair of contrasting traits

k. offspring of the F_1 generation

l. when the two alleles of a particular gene are the same

m. branch of biology that studies heredity

n. different versions of a gene

o. offspring of the P generation

p. set of alleles that an individual has

Vocabulary Review continued

Write the correct term from the list below in the space next to its definition.

codominance   pedigree   Punnett square
incomplete dominance   polygenic trait   sex-linked trait
multiple alleles   probability   test cross

_____ **17.** diagram that predicts the outcomes of a genetic cross

_____ **18.** cross of a homozygous recessive individual with an individual with a dominant phenotype of unknown genotype

_____ **19.** the likelihood that a specific event will occur

_____ **20.** a family history that shows how a trait is inherited

_____ **21.** trait whose allele is located on the X chromosome

_____ **22.** when several genes influence a trait

_____ **23.** when an individual displays a trait that is intermediate between the two parents

_____ **24.** two dominant alleles are expressed at the same time

_____ **25.** genes with three or more alleles

Assessment

Test Prep Pretest

In the space provided, write the letter of the term or phrase that best completes each statement or best answers each question.

_____ 1. *Pisum sativum*, the garden pea, is a good subject to use in studying heredity for all of the following reasons EXCEPT
   a. Several varieties of *Pisum sativum* are available that differ in easily distinguishable traits.
   b. *Pisum sativum* is a small, easy-to-grow plant.
   c. *Pisum sativum* matures quickly and produces a large number of offspring.
   d. A *Pisum sativum* plant with male reproductive parts must cross-pollinate with a plant having female reproductive parts for reproduction to take place.

_____ 2. Step 1 of Mendel's garden pea experiment, allowing each variety of garden pea to self-pollinate for several generations, produced the
   a. F_1 generation.   **c.** P generation.
   b. F_2 generation.   **d.** P_2 generation.

_____ 3. In the F_2 generation in Mendel's experiments, the ratio of dominant to recessive phenotypes was
   a. 1:3.   **c.** 2:1.
   b. 1:2.   **d.** 3:1.

_____ 4. The trait that was expressed in the F_1 generation in Mendel's experiment is considered
   a. recessive.   **c.** second filial.
   b. dominant.   **d.** parental.

_____ 5. Mendel's law of segregation states that
   a. pairs of alleles are dependent on one another when separation occurs during gamete formation.
   b. pairs of alleles separate independently of one another after gamete formation.
   c. each pair of alleles remains together when gametes are formed.
   d. the two alleles for a trait separate when gametes are formed.

_____ 6. A series of genetic crosses results in 787 long-stemmed plants and 277 short-stemmed plants. The probability that you will obtain short-stemmed plants if you repeat this experiment is
   a. $\frac{277}{1,064}$.   **c.** $\frac{787}{277}$.

   b. $\frac{277}{787}$.   **d.** $\frac{787}{1,064}$.

_____ **7.** Crossing a snapdragon that has red flowers with one that has white flowers produces a snapdragon that has pink flowers. The trait for flower color exhibits
  a. multiple alleles.
  b. complete dominance.
  c. incomplete dominance.
  d. codominance.

_____ **8.** Which of the following is NOT considered a genetic disorder?
  a. sickle cell anemia
  b. hemophilia
  c. AIDS
  d. cystic fibrosis

_____ **9.** On which of the following chromosomes would a sex-linked trait most likely be found in humans?
  a. X
  b. Y
  c. O
  d. YO

_____ **10.** The roan color of a horse is an example of
  a. homozygous alleles.
  b. codominance.
  c. incomplete dominance.
  d. Both (a) and (c)

Questions 11 and 12 refer to the figure at right, which represents a monohybrid cross between two individuals that are heterozygous for a trait.

	D	*d*
D	*DD*	*Dd*
__	*D__*	*d__*

_____ **11.** If the resulting phenotypic ratio is 3:1, the missing parental allele is
  a. *d*.
  b. *D*.
  c. *Dd*.
  d. *DD*.

_____ **12.** The two unknown genotypes in the offspring are
  a. *DD* and *dd*.
  b. *Dd* and *Dd*.
  c. *dd* and *DD*.
  d. *Dd* and *dd*.

_____ **13.** Which of the following summarizes one of Mendel's major hypotheses developed from his studies of garden peas?
  a. All of an individual's alleles make up its genotype.
  b. Traits that are intermediate between two parents are caused by genes that are incompletely dominant.
  c. There are alternative versions of genes, which are called alleles today.
  d. When two dominant alleles are expressed together, they are called codominant.

_____ **14.** Which of the following is an example of a test cross?
  a. *YY* × *YY*
  b. *YY* × *yy*
  c. *Yy* × *Yy*
  d. All of the above

Test Prep Pretest *continued*

_____**15.** What is the goal of genetic counseling?
  a. to cure genetic disorders
  b. to inform people about genetic disorders that could affect them or their offspring
  c. to use gene technology to correct certain genetic disorders
  d. to identify people who have a family history of genetic disorders

Question 16 refers to the figure below, which shows the inheritance of sickle cell anemia in a family.

_____**16.** Which of the following is true based on the information provided in the pedigree?
  a. Both parents have sickle cell anemia.
  b. Both parents carry an allele for sickle cell anemia.
  c. Sickle cell anemia is caused by a dominant allele.
  d. All three children are carriers of a defective gene that causes sickle cell anemia.

Complete each statement by writing the correct term or phrase in the space provided.

17. The investigator whose studies formed the basis of modern genetics is

_____ .

18. The _____ , or physical appearance, of an individual is

determined by the alleles that code for traits. The set of alleles that an individ-

ual has is called its _____ .

19. A cross between a pea plant that is true-breeding for green pod color and one that is true breeding for yellow pod color is an example of

a(n) _____ cross.

Test Prep Pretest *continued*

20. Characteristics such as eye color, height, weight, and hair and skin color are

examples of _____ _____ because
several genes act together to influence a trait.

21. Mutations in genetic material may cause _____

_____, such as cystic fibrosis and muscular dystrophy.

Read each question, and write your answer in the space provided.

22. What approximate ratio of plants expressing contrasting traits did Mendel
calculate in his F_2 generation of garden peas? What steps did he take to
calculate this ratio?

_____

_____

_____

_____

23. Name Mendel's two laws of heredity.

_____

_____

24. Give an example of how the environment might influence gene expression.

_____

_____

_____

25. Describe one sex-linked genetic disorder.

_____

_____

_____

Name _____ Class _____ Date _____

Vocabulary Review

Complete the crossword puzzle using the clues provided.

ACROSS

2. five-carbon sugar found in DNA nucleotides

3. enzyme that adds nucleotides to exposed nitrogen bases

4. substance prepared from killed or weakened microorganisms

6. change in phenotype of bacteria caused by the presence of foreign genetic material

8. The term *double* _____ is used to describe the shape of DNA.

10. a virus that infects bacteria

11. enzyme that separates DNA by breaking the hydrogen bonds that link the nitrogen bases

12. name for DNA subunit

DOWN

1. relationship of two DNA strands to each other

4. disease-causing

5. Base-_____ rules describe the arrangement of the nitrogen bases between two DNA strands.

7. the process by which DNA is copied

9. A replication _____ is the area that results after the double helix separates during replication.

Test Prep Pretest

Complete each statement by writing the correct term or phrase in the space provided.

1. In 1928, Frederick Griffith found that the capsule that enclosed one strain of *Streptococcus pneumoniae* caused the microorganism's

   _____ .

2. Avery's experiments demonstrated that DNA is the _____ material.

3. After infecting *Escherichia coli* bacteria with ^{32}P-labeled phages, Hershey and Chase traced the ^{32}P. The scientists found most of the radioactive substance

   in the _____ .

4. Watson and Crick used the X-ray _____ photographs of Wilkins and Franklin to build their model of DNA.

5. The process of making new DNA is called _____ .

6. The point at which the double helix separates during replication is called

   the _____ _____ .

7. DNA replication occurs during the _____ phase of the cell cycle.

8. Eukaryotic DNA contains many replication forks working in concert,

   whereas prokaryotic DNA contains only _____ replication forks during replication.

In the space provided, write the letter of the description that best matches the term or phrase.

_____ **9.** transformation

_____ **10.** replication

_____ **11.** DNA helicase

_____ **12.** Wilkins and Franklin

_____ **13.** Watson and Crick

_____ **14.** DNA polymerase

_____ **15.** Avery

_____ **16.** Griffith

a. discovered the three-dimensional structure of DNA with the help of other scientists

b. proofreads DNA during replication

c. developed high quality X-ray diffraction photographs of DNA

d. results in two DNA molecules that are identical to the original DNA molecule

e. results in a change in a cell's genotype

f. demonstrated that DNA is the material responsible for transformation

g. discovered transformation in bacterial cells

h. unwinds the two DNA strands during replication

Read each question, and write your answer in the space provided.

17. Relate the role of base-pairing rules to the structure of DNA.

_____

_____

_____

_____

18. Describe the components of a nucleotide.

_____

_____

_____

19. What happened when Griffith mixed harmless living *R* bacteria with harmless heat-killed *S* bacteria and then injected mice with this mixture?

_____

_____

_____

_____

20. How did Avery's experiment identify the material responsible for transformation?

_____

_____

_____

_____

_____

21. Why did Hershey and Chase use radioactive elements in their experiments?

_____

_____

_____

_____

22. Explain how DNA polymerase "proofreads" a new DNA strand.

_____

_____

_____

_____

_____

23. Describe the role of DNA helicases during replication.

_____

_____

_____

_____

_____

Test Prep Pretest *continued*

Questions 24 and 25 refer to the figure below.

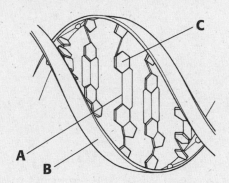

24. What does the figure above represent?

_____

_____

25. Identify the structures labeled *A–C.*

_____

_____

Name _____ Class _____ Date _____

Vocabulary Review

Complete the crossword puzzle using the clues provided.

ACROSS

1. Like DNA, _____ acid (RNA) is a molecule made of nucleotides linked together.

2. RNA _____ is an enzyme involved in transcription.

3. The type of RNA that carries the instructions for making a protein from a gene to the site of translation is called _____ RNA.

4. The entire process by which proteins are made is called _____ expression.

6. process for transferring a gene's instructions for making a protein to an mRNA molecule

10. a three-nucleotide sequence on the mRNA that specifies an amino acid or "start" or "stop" signal

12. piece of DNA that serves as an on-off switch for transcription

14. long segment of nucleotides on a eukaryotic gene that has no coding information

DOWN

1. a protein that binds to an operator and inhibits transcription

5. portion of a eukaryotic gene that is translated

6. a process that puts together the amino acids that make up a protein

7. a three-nucleotide sequence on a tRNA that is complementary to one of the codons of the genetic code

8. RNA molecules that are part of the structure of ribosomes are called _____ RNA.

9. RNA molecules that temporarily carry a specific amino acid on one end are called _____ RNA.

11. The _____ code specifies the amino acids and "start" and "stop" signals with their codon.

13. collective name for a group of genes involved in the same function, their promoter site, and their operator

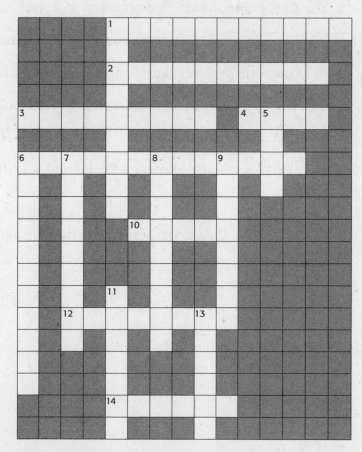

Name _____ Class _____ Date _____

Test Prep Pretest

Complete each statement by writing the correct term or phrase in the space provided.

1. Instead of the base thymine found in DNA, RNA has a base called

   _____ .

2. Transcription begins when an enzyme called _____

   _____ binds to the beginning of a gene on a region of

   DNA called a promoter.

3. The instructions for building a protein are written as a series of three-

   nucleotide sequences called _____ .

4. During translation, the area of the ribosome called the

   _____ site receives the next tRNA molecule.

5. Because of its position on the operon, the _____ is able
   to control RNA polymerase's access to the structural genes.

6. The *lac* operon is switched off when a protein called a(n)

   _____ is bound to the operator.

7. In eukaryotic gene regulation, proteins called _____

   _____ help arrange RNA polymerases in the correct

   position on the promoter.

8. In eukaryotes, long segments of nucleotides with no coding information

   are called _____ .

9. In eukaryotes, the portions of a gene that are actually translated into

   proteins are called _____ .

10. Insertions, deletions and point mutations are types of _____

   _____ .

Test Prep Pretest *continued*

Questions 11–13 refer to the figure below.

DNA   RNA   Protein

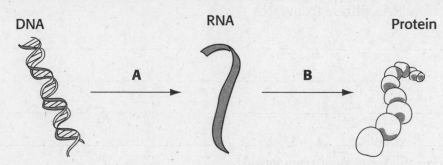

11. The processing of information from DNA into proteins, as shown above, is

referred to as _____ _____ .

12. Stage *A* is called _____ .

13. Stage *B* is called _____ .

In the space provided, write the letter of the term or phrase that best completes each statement or best answers each question.

_____14. In what kinds of cells do mutations occur?
    a. body cells   **c.** reproductive cells
    b. gametes   **d.** All of the above

_____15. A mutation that moves a gene to a new location is called a(n)
    a. point mutation.   **c.** transposon.
    b. insertion.   **d.** deletion.

_____16. Which of the following represents the codons that correspond to this
    segment of DNA: TATCAGGAT?
    a. AUA—GUC—CUA   **c.** AUAGU—CCUA
    b. ATA—GTC—CTA   **d.** ACA—CUC—GUA

_____17. Which of the following are the anticodons that correspond to the
    mRNA codons CAG—ACU—UUU?
    a. GTC—TGA—AAA
    b. GUC—UGA—AAA
    c. glutamine—threonine—phenylalanine
    d. GAC—UCA—AAA

_____18. Because the genetic code is the same in all organisms, it appears that
    a. the genetic code evolved more than once.
    b. the codon GUC codes for different proteins in different organisms.
    c. thymine will soon replace uracil in RNA.
    d. all life-forms have a common ancestor.

▌Test Prep Pretest *continued*

Read each question, and write your answer in the space provided.

19. Explain how RNA differs from DNA.

_____

_____

_____

_____

20. Summarize the process of translation.

_____

_____

_____

21. Describe the functions of RNA.

_____

_____

_____

_____

_____

_____

22. What is the *lac* operon?

_____

_____

23. Explain why gene regulation in eukaryotic cells is more complex than in prokaryotic cells.

_____

_____

_____

_____

Test Prep Pretest *continued*

24. Why do scientists think that introns and exons contribute to evolutionary flexibility?

_____

_____

_____

_____

25. Describe the three ways that mutation can alter genetic material.

_____

_____

_____

_____

_____

Skills Worksheet

Vocabulary Review

Unscramble each listed term, and write the correct term in the space at right. In the space at left, write the letter of the description below that best matches the term or phrase.

_____ **1.** nmauH nmeeGo tjPceor _____

_____ **2.** tveorc _____

_____ **3.** smipdal _____

_____ **4.** brtnneacimo DAN _____

_____ **5.** ccveina _____

_____ **6.** ttiicrneosr meenyzs _____

_____ **7.** gtnrcnaeis aailmn _____

_____ **8.** neeg gninolc _____

_____ **9.** ssierhpocrteelo _____

_____ **10.** raeicngsnt aaimnl _____

_____ **11.** eegncit ggeeiinnren _____

a. animal that has foreign DNA in its cells

b. a solution containing a weakened or modified version of a pathogen

c. a research effort to determine the nucleotide sequence of the human genome and map the location of every gene

d. an animal that has foreign DNA in its cells

e. bacterial enzymes that recognize and bind to specific short sequences of DNA, then cut the DNA at specific sites within the sequences

f. a technique that uses an electrical field within a gel to separate molecules by their size and charge

g. a circular DNA molecule that can replicate independently of the main chromosomes of bacteria

h. an agent that is used to carry the gene of interest into another cell

i. DNA made from two or more different organisms

j. when copies of the gene of interest are made each time the host cell reproduces

k. the process of manipulating genes for practical purposes

Skills Worksheet
Test Prep Pretest

In the space provided, write the letter of the term or phrase that best completes each statement or best answers each question.

_____ 1. How are genetically engineered vaccines different from those made from weakened pathogens?
  a. They are ineffective.
  b. They cause only a mild form of the disease.
  c. They eliminate the risk of transmitting the disease to the person injected.
  d. They cause the immune system to make antibodies.

_____ 2. Tetracycline is used in genetic engineering experiments as a way to
  a. identify bacteria that have taken up the recombined plasmid.
  b. produce stronger strains of bacteria.
  c. prevent the cultures from becoming infected with bacteria.
  d. kill cell clones that contain recombinant DNA.

_____ 3. Which genes of a pathogen are used to make a genetically engineered vaccine?
  a. those that encode a pathogen's surface proteins
  b. those that are harmless
  c. those that are similar to human genes
  d. those that encode antibodies

_____ 4. Gene technology is used to improve farm animals in which of the following ways?
  a. increasing milk production using cow growth hormone produced by bacteria
  b. cloning herds of animals to make medically useful human proteins
  c. producing milk containing human proteins by adding human genes to farm-animal genes
  d. All of the above

Questions 5–7 refer to the figure below, which shows the steps of a genetic engineering experiment using DNA from a human insulin gene.

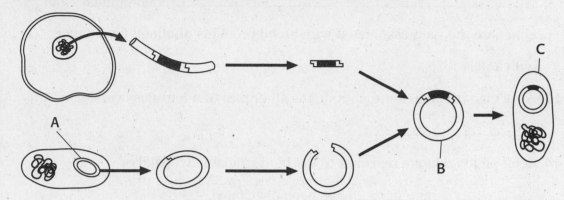

_____ **5.** The structure labeled *A* is called
    a. plasmid DNA.
    b. a vector.
    c. a restriction enzyme.
    d. Both (a) and (b)

_____ **6.** In *B*, the DNA of the gene and the vector are
    a. cloned.
    b. isolated.
    c. recombined.
    d. cut by the restriction enzyme.

_____ **7.** In *C*, the
    a. gene is cloned.
    b. cells are screened.
    c. recombined plasmid DNA is inserted into the bacterium.
    d. DNA is cut.

Complete each statement by writing the correct term or phrase in the space provided.

8. The first step of Cohen and Boyer's genetic engineering experiment was to

isolate the _____ of interest from the DNA of an African

clawed frog.

9. Recombinant DNA is made when a DNA fragment is put into the DNA of a(n)

_____ .

10. Any two fragments of DNA cut by the same restriction enzyme can pair

because their ends are _____ .

11. Genetic engineering has benefited humans afflicted with diabetes by

developing bacteria that produce _____ .

12. By using the genetically engineered blood-clotting agent

_____ _____ , hemophiliacs can

eliminate the risks associated with blood products obtained from other

individuals.

13. A vaccine is a solution that contains all or part of a harmless version of a(n)

_____ .

14. Crop plants that are resistant to the biodegradable weedkiller

_____ have been developed.

15. In genetic engineering, the enzyme _____

_____ helps the DNA fragments bind.

Read each question, and write your answer in the space provided.

16. Describe the Human Genome Project.

_____

_____

_____

_____

17. List two ways in which DNA fingerprints are used.

_____

_____

_____

18. Explain why the development of genetically engineered proteins has been
important to pharmaceutical companies.

_____

_____

_____

_____

_____

_____

Test Prep Pretest *continued*

19. Why is the development of plants that are resistant to insects important?

_____

_____

_____

20. Explain the first step of Ian Wilmut's successful cloning experiment.

_____

_____

_____

_____

_____

_____

_____

_____

Skills Worksheet

Vocabulary Review

In the space provided, explain how the terms in each pair differ in meaning.

1. radioisotope, half-life

_____

_____

_____

_____

2. fossil, cyanobacteria

_____

_____

_____

_____

3. eubacteria, archaebacteria

_____

_____

_____

_____

4. mycorrhiza, mutualism

_____

_____

_____

_____

Vocabulary Review *continued*

In the space provided, write the letter of the description that best matches the term or phrase.

_____ 5. radiometric dating

_____ 6. endosymbiosis

_____ 7. protists

_____ 8. mass extinction

_____ 9. arthropod

_____ 10. vertebrate

_____ 11. continental drift

_____ 12. microsphere

a. animal with hard outer skeleton and jointed limbs

b. the movement of Earth's land masses over geologic time

c. animals with backbones

d. calculation of the age of an object by measuring the proportions of radio-active isotopes of certain elements

e. tiny droplets made of short chains of amino acids

f. the theory that mitochondria and chloroplasts are the descendants of symbiotic aerobic eubacteria

g. members of a kingdom of unicellular and multicellular eukaryotic organisms

h. the death of all members of many different species

Skills Worksheet

Test Prep Pretest

In the space provided, write the letter of the term or phrase that best completes each statement or best answers each question.

_____ **1.** Radiometric dating has determined that Earth is approximately
    a. 4,000 years old.   **c.** 2.5 billion years old.
    b. 500,000 years old.   **d.** 4.5 billion years old.

_____ **2.** A mechanism for heredity was necessary in order to begin
    a. microspheres.   **c.** RNA.
    b. life.   **d.** protein.

_____ **3.** The kingdoms that evolved from protists are
    a. eubacteria, fungi, and animals.
    b. archaebacteria, plants, and animals.
    c. eubacteria, plants, and animals.
    d. fungi, plants, and animals.

_____ **4.** Life was able to move from the sea to land because
    a. photosynthesis by cyanobacteria added oxygen
        to Earth's atmosphere.
    b. ozone was created from the oxygen produced by photosynthesis.
    c. ozone provides a shield from the harsh ultraviolet rays
        of the sun.
    d. All of the above

_____ **5.** Louis Lerman's bubble model addresses the problem of
    a. lightning.
    b. ultraviolet radiation damage to ammonia and methane.
    c. volcanic heat.
    d. a dense ozone layer.

_____ **6.** The following animals are all arthropods.
    a. crabs, lobsters, insects, and spiders
    b. crabs, snakes, insects, and spiders
    c. frogs, toads, and salamanders
    d. frogs, toads, salamanders, and snakes

_____ **7.** The primordial soup model requires
    a. the sun, electrical energy, or volcanic eruptions.
    b. at least 1 billion years.
    c. hydrogen-containing gases.
    d. All of the above

| Test Prep Pretest *continued*

_____ **8.** Amphibians were able to adapt to life on land for all of the following reasons EXCEPT
   a. lungs.
   b. watertight skin.
   c. limbs.
   d. a platform of bone that provided a base for the limbs to work against.

_____ **9.** Reptiles are more completely adapted to land than amphibians are because reptiles
   a. have watertight skin.
   b. can lay their eggs on dry land.
   c. do not have to live near the water.
   d. All of the above

_____ **10.** Scientists think the first step toward cellular organization was
   a. nucleotides.   **c.** microspheres.
   b. coacervates.   **d.** RNA enzymes.

In the space provided, write the letter of the description that best matches the term or phrase.

_____ **11.** bacteria

_____ **12.** mass extinctions

_____ **13.** plants and fungi

_____ **14.** RNA

_____ **15.** jawless fishes

_____ **16.** endosymbiosis

_____ **17.** multicellularity

_____ **18.** continental drift

a. the first self-replicating information storage molecule

b. thought to have evolved 2.5 billion years ago

c. cause decreased competition for resources among survivors

d. the first multicellular organisms to live on land

e. enabled cell specialization

f. explains why related animals are found on continents separated by oceans

g. the first vertebrates

h. the theory that mitochondria and chloroplasts are descendants of symbiotic, aerobic eubacteria

Complete each statement by writing the correct term or phrase in the space provided.

19. In Louis Lerman's model, the hydrogen-containing gases needed to make

amino acids were trapped in _____ _____ .

20. The earliest stages of cellular organization may have been the formation of

_____ .

21. Because of the mass extinction at the end of the Permian period, about

96 percent of all species of _____ living at the time became
extinct.

22. A partnership, such as the one found in mycorrhizae, in which each organism

helps the other survive is called _____ .

23. The first group of animals to live on land was the _____ .

Read each question, and write your answer in the space provided.

24. Why was the development of multicellular organisms a great step forward in
the evolution of life on Earth?

_____

_____

25. What were the first vertebrates to live on land? What structural changes
enabled them to make the transition?

_____

_____

_____

_____

_____

_____

Skills Worksheet)

Vocabulary Review

In the space provided, write the letter of the term or phrase that best completes each statement or best answers each question.

_____ 1. The process in which organisms with traits well suited to an environment are more likely to survive and to produce offspring is
   a. trait mechanisms.   c. genetic principles.
   b. origin of species.   d. natural selection.

_____ 2. In biology, all of the individuals of a species that live together in one place at one time are called a
   a. population.   c. half-life.
   b. community.   d. habitat.

_____ 3. A change in the genetic makeup of species over time is called
   a. radioactive dating.   c. camouflage.
   b. evolution.   d. natural selection.

_____ 4. The process by which a species becomes better suited to its environment is
   a. industrialization.   c. adaptation.
   b. not an advantage.   d. destructive to its survival.

_____ 5. Structures that share a common ancestry or are similar because they are modified versions of structures from a common ancestor are
   a. not related.   c. not homologous.
   b. homologous.   d. young in origin.

_____ 6. Structures with no function that are remnants of an organism's evolutionary past are
   a. not visible on organisms.   c. vestigial.
   b. young in origin.   d. useful to the organism.

_____ 7. The accumulation of differences between species or populations is called
   a. gradualism.   c. divergence.
   b. punctuated equilibrium.   d. observational species.

_____ 8. The hypothesis that evolution of a species occurs in periods of rapid change separated by periods of little or no change is called
   a. divergence.   c. isolation.
   b. gradualism.   d. punctuated equilibrium.

_____ 9. Populations of the same species that differ genetically because they have adapted to different living conditions are
   a. observational species.   c. subspecies.
   b. different species.   d. conditional races.

Vocabulary Review *continued*

_____10. The hypothesis that the evolution of different species occurs at a slow constant rate is called
 a. punctuated equilibrium.   **c.** divergence.
 b. gradualism.   **d.** transitionism.

_____11. The condition in which two populations of the same species CANNOT breed with one another is called reproductive
 a. infertility.   **c.** isolation.
 b. extinction.   **d.** selection.

_____12. When a species permanently disappears, the species is said to be
 a. extinct.   **c.** mutated.
 b. isolated.   **d.** eliminated.

_____13. Antibiotic resistance in bacteria is called
 a. natural selection.   **c.** divergence.
 b. gradualism.   **d.** speciation.

_____14. The process by which new species form is called
 a. biological change.   **c.** speciation.
 b. reproduction.   **d.** divergence.

_____15. The inability of formerly interbreeding groups to mate or produce fertile offspring is called
 a. sterility.   **c.** reproductive isolation.
 b. divergence.   **d.** extinction.

_____16. A scientist who studies fossils is called a(n)
 a. archaeologist.   **c.** paleontologist.
 b. ecologist.   **d.** biologist.

_____17. In Grants' study, the effect of weather on the size of the finch's beak is an example of
 a. isolation.   **c.** gradualism.
 b. natural selection.   **d.** fossilization.

_____18. Biological molecules that are considered evidence for evolution include
 a. DNA.   **c.** proteins.
 b. amino acids.   **d.** All of the above

Name _____ Class _____ Date _____

Test Prep Pretest

In the space provided, write the letter of the term or phrase that best completes each statement or best answers each question.

_____ 1. On the Galápagos Islands, Darwin saw that the plants and animals closely resembled those of the
    a. islands off the coast of North America.
    b. coast of South America.
    c. islands off the coast of Africa.
    d. coast of South Africa.

_____ 2. Which of the following is a factor in natural selection?
    a. Individuals of a species compete with one another to survive.
    b. All species are genetically diverse.
    c. Individuals better able to adapt to changes leave more offspring.
    d. All of the above

_____ 3. When the individuals of two populations can no longer interbreed, the two populations are considered to be
    a. different families.   **c.** the same species.
    b. different species.   **d.** unrelated.

_____ 4. The fossil record provides evidence that
    a. older species gave rise to more-recent species.
    b. all species were formed during Earth's formation and have changed little since then.
    c. the fossilized species have no connection to today's species.
    d. fossils cannot be dated.

_____ 5. Comparing human hemoglobin with the hemoglobin of gorillas, mice, chickens, and frogs reveals that humans have the fewest amino acid differences with
    a. gorillas.   **c.** chickens.
    b. mice.   **d.** frogs.

_____ 6. Individuals that are better able to cope with the challenges of their environment tend to
    a. decrease in population over time.
    b. leave more offspring than those more suited to the environment.
    c. leave fewer offspring than those less suited to the environment.
    d. leave more offspring than those less suited to the environment.

_____ 7. Which factor does NOT play a role in determining the beak size of Galápagos finches?
    a. amount of food available   **c.** size of the bird
    b. seed size   **d.** weather

_____ 8. Members of different subspecies
    a. are considered to be different species.
    b. differ genetically because of adaptations for different living conditions.
    c. can no longer interbreed successfully.
    d. will never diverge to become different species.

Questions 9 and 10 refer to the figures below.

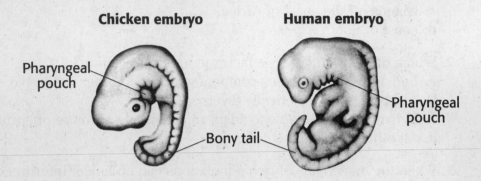

_____ 9. Which of the following statements best reflects the evolutionary importance of the figures above?
    a. New genetic instructions have been disregarded in the evolution of vertebrates.
    b. Early in development, vertebrate embryos show no evidence of common ancestry.
    c. The evolutionary history of organisms is seen in the way embryos develop.
    d. All adult vertebrates retain pharyngeal pouches.

_____ 10. Which of the following statements is NOT true about the vertebrate embryos shown above?
    a. Each embryo develops a tail.
    b. Each embryo has buds that become limbs.
    c. Each embryo has pharyngeal pouches.
    d. Each embryo has fur.

Test Prep Pretest *continued*

Complete each statement by writing the correct term or phrase in the space provided.

11. Over time, change within species leads to the replacement of old species by

    new species as less successful species become _____ .

12. While on the *Beagle*, Darwin read *Principles of Geology*, which contained a

    detailed account of _____ theory of evolution.

13. The changing of a species that results in its being better suited to its

    environment is called _____ .

14. A(n) _____ is a group of individuals that belong to the
    same species, live in a defined area, and breed with others in the group.

15. The condition in which two populations of the same species are separated

    from one another is called _____ .

16. Species that shared a common ancestor in the recent past have many

    _____ _____ or

    _____ sequence similarities.

17. Given that the forelimbs of all vertebrates share the same basic arrangement

    of bones, forelimbs are said to be _____ structures.

18. The _____ of individuals who adapt to changing condi-
    tions tend to increase over time.

19. The model of evolution in which gradual change leads to species formation

    over time is called _____ .

20. A whale's pelvic bones are _____ structures because they
    no longer function like the pelvis of a land vertebrate.

21. Darwin felt that fossils of extinct armadillos that resembled living armadillos

    were evidence that _____ is a(n)

    _____ process.

22. The accumulation of differences between groups such as populations,

    species, and genera is _____ .

Test Prep Pretest *continued*

Read each question, and write your answer in the space provided.

23. What was Lamarck's hypothesis regarding evolution?

_____

_____

_____

24. Briefly explain the importance of Thomas Malthus's essay on the growth of the human population to Darwin's theory of evolution.

_____

_____

_____

25. Briefly summarize the modern version of Darwin's theory of evolution by natural selection.

_____

_____

_____

_____

_____

_____

Skills Worksheet

Vocabulary Review

Complete each statement by writing the correct term or phrase from the list below in the space provided.

analogous character	convergent evolution	kingdom
binomial nomenclature	derived characters	order
biological species	domain	phylogenetic tree
cladistics	evolutionary systematics	phylogeny
cladogram	family	phylum
class	genus	taxonomy

1. The classification level in which classes with similar characteristics are

   grouped is called a(n) _____ .

2. When taxonomists give varying subjective degrees of importance to characters, they are applying _____ _____ .

3. Reconstructing phylogenies by inferring relationships based on similarities

   derived from a common ancestor without considering the "strength" of a

   character is called _____ .

4. The evolutionary history of a species is its _____ .

5. Orders with common properties are combined into a(n)

   _____ .

6. Similar families are combined into a(n) _____ .

7. The classification level in which similar genera are grouped is called a(n)

   _____ .

8. A similar feature that evolved through convergent evolution is called a(n)

   _____ _____ .

9. In _____ _____ , organisms evolve

   similar features independently, often because they live in similar habitats.

10. A(n) _____ is a branching diagram used to show evolutionary relationships in groups of shared derived characters.

11. The most general level of classification is _____ .

| Vocabulary Review *continued*

12. A(n) _____ is a taxonomic category containing similar species.

13. Linnaeus developed a system for naming and classifying organisms, which is

called _____ .

14. A(n) _____ _____ is a group of interbreeding or potentially interbreeding natural populations that are reproductively isolated from other such groups.

15. Unique characteristics used in cladistics are called _____

_____ .

16. The two-word system for naming organisms is called _____

_____ .

17. A(n) _____ contains many phyla.

18. In evolutionary systematics, evolutionary relationships are displayed in a

branching diagram called a _____ _____ .

Skills Worksheet

Test Prep Pretest

In the space provided, write the letter of the term or phrase that best completes each statement or best answers each question.

_____ 1. In one of the earliest classification systems, Aristotle grouped plants and animals according to
   a. basic categories.
   b. structural similarities.
   c. genus.
   d. major characteristics.

_____ 2. Although Linnaeus used the Latin polynomial system in his books, he created his own
   a. rules of grammar.
   b. taxonomic categories.
   c. evolutionary systematics.
   d. two-word shorthand system, also in Latin.

_____ 3. Scientists classify organisms by studying their forms and
   a. structures.
   b. size.
   c. method of reproduction.
   d. cladograms.

_____ 4. Cladograms determine evolutionary relationships between organisms by examining
   a. the strength of a character.
   b. the degree of difference between organisms.
   c. shared ancestral characters.
   d. shared derived characters.

_____ 5. All members of the kingdom Animalia are multicellular
   a. autotrophs whose cells have walls.
   b. heterotrophs whose cells have walls.
   c. heterotrophs whose cells lack walls.
   d. autotrophs whose cells lack walls.

_____ 6. Biological species, as defined by Ernst Mayr,
   a. are closely related.
   b. are interbreeding natural populations.
   c. produce infertile offspring.
   d. produce infertile hybrids.

_____ 7. The characteristics that scientists use in cladistics are
   a. analogous structures.
   b. shared derived characters.
   c. convergent structures.
   d. shared homologous traits.

| Test Prep Pretest *continued*

_____ **8.** Bird wings and insect wings are
  a. homologous traits.   **c.** analogous traits.
  b. derived traits.   **d.** phylogenetic traits.

_____ **9.** The biological species concept cannot be applied to
  a. species that can produce fertile hybrids.
  b. all bacteria.
  c. species that reproduce asexually.
  d. All of the above

_____ **10.** Scientific names
  a. must have three Latin words and correct Latin grammar.
  b. include the genus and family.
  c. have rules established by British and American biologists.
  d. enable biologists to communicate regardless of their native language.

_____ **11.** Which of the following lists the eight classification levels in proper descending order?
  a. domain, kingdom, phylum, class, order, family, genus, species
  b. kingdom, domain, phylum, order, class, family, genus, species
  c. kingdom, phylum, family, class, domain, order, genus, species
  d. phylum, kingdom, domain, class, order, family, genus, species

_____ **12.** The scientific naming system requires all of the following EXCEPT that
  a. both words should be underlined or italicized.
  b. the genus is to be capitalized.
  c. the species should be the second word.
  d. the genus is never abbreviated.

Complete each statement by writing the correct term or phrase in the space provided.

13. The naming system developed by Linnaeus is called _____

  _____ .

14. One genus can include several _____ .

15. Ernst Mayr developed the concept that a(n) _____

  _____ is reproductively isolated from other groups.

16. When _____ _____ are incomplete, closely related species can produce hybrids.

17. The biological species concept works best for most members of the kingdom

  _____ .

18. Similar features in organisms that do not share a recent common ancestor are

called _____ _____ .

19. Scientists use evidence of _____ characters to recon-
struct evolutionary history.

20. The evolutionary history of a species is called its _____ .

Read each question, and write your answer in the space provided.

21. Explain the difference between homologous characters and analogous
characters. Give an example of each.

_____

_____

_____

_____

_____

_____

_____

22. Which classification system would probably be used first if a scientist
discovered five unknown plants? Explain.

_____

_____

_____

23. Explain why Mayr's concept of biological species has limited applications.

_____

_____

_____

_____

Test Prep Pretest *continued*

Questions 24 and 25 refer to the figure below. The phylogenetic tree shown indicates the evolutionary relationships for a hypothetical group of modern organisms, labeled *1–5*, and their ancestors, labeled *A–E*.

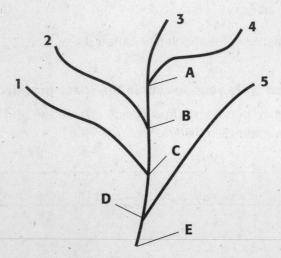

24. Which two modern organisms are likely to be most closely related?

_____

25. What was the most recent common ancestor of the organisms labeled *1* and *5*?

_____

_____

Skills Worksheet

Vocabulary Review

Complete each statement by writing the correct term or phrase from the list below in the space provided.

carrying capacity	genetic drift	population
density-dependent factors	Hardy-Weinberg principle	population density
density-independent factors	*K*-strategists	population model
directional selection	logistic model	population size
dispersion	nonrandom mating	*r*-strategists
exponential growth curve	normal distribution	stabilizing selection
gene flow	polygenic trait	

1. A(n) _____ consists of all the individuals of a species that

live together in one place at one time.

2. One of the most important features of any population is its _____

_____ , the number of individuals in a population.

3. A second important feature of a population is _____

_____ , the number of individuals that live in a given area.

4. A third feature of populations is _____ , which refers to

the way the individuals of the population are arranged in space.

5. When demographers try to predict how a population will grow, they use a(n)

_____ _____ , a hypothetical

population that exhibits the key characteristics of a real population.

6. When the rate of population growth stays the same and population size is

plotted against time on a graph, the population growth curve resembles a

J-shaped curve called a(n) _____ _____

_____ .

7. The population that an environment can sustain is called the

_____ _____ .

| Vocabulary Review *continued*

8. As populations grow, limited resources get used up. These resources are

called _____-_____

_____ because the rate at which they become depleted

depends on the density of the population that uses them.

9. The _____ _____ is a population
growth model in which exponential growth is limited by a density-dependent
factor.

10. Many species of plants and insects reproduce rapidly. Their growth is usually

limited by environmental conditions, also known as _____-

_____ _____ .

11. Many of these species grow exponentially when environmental conditions

permit their reproduction. Such species are called _____ .

12. Slow-growing populations, such as whales and redwood trees, are called

_____ because their population density is usually near

the carrying capacity (K) of their environment.

13. According to the _____-_____

_____ , the frequencies of alleles in a population do not

change unless evolutionary forces act on the population.

14. The evolutionary forces include the mutation of genes and

_____ _____ , which is the

movement of alleles into or out of a population.

15. Sometimes individuals prefer to mate with others that live nearby or are of

their own phenotype, a situation called _____

_____ .

16. In small populations, the frequency of an allele can be greatly changed by a

chance event, such as a fire or landslide. This change in allele frequency is

called _____ _____ .

▌Vocabulary Review *continued*

17. A trait that is influenced by several genes is called a(n)

_____ _____ .

18. If you were to plot the height of everyone in your class on a graph, the values

would probably form a hill-shaped curve called a(n) _____

_____ .

19. When selection causes the frequency of a particular trait to move in one

direction, this form of selection is called _____

_____ .

20. When selection eliminates extremes at both ends of a range of phenotypes,

the frequencies of the intermediate phenotypes increase. This form of

selection is called _____ _____ .

Assessment

Test Prep Pretest

In the space provided, write the letter of the term or phrase that best completes each statement or best answers each question.

_____ 1. The three main patterns of dispersion in a population are
   a. nonrandomly spaced, evenly spaced, and clumped distribution.
   b. nonrandomly spaced, evenly spaced, and unevenly spaced.
   c. randomly spaced, evenly spaced, and clumped distribution.
   d. randomly spaced, evenly spaced, and unevenly spaced.

_____ 2. In the exponential model of population growth, the growth rate
   a. remains constant.   **c.** rises.
   b. declines.   **d.** rises and then declines.

_____ 3. *K*-strategists tend to live in environments that are
   a. unstable.   **c.** unpredictable.
   b. rapidly changing.   **d.** stable and predictable.

_____ 4. The Hardy-Weinberg principle
   a. can predict genotype frequencies affected by evolutionary forces.
   b. can predict genetic drift.
   c. applies only to large populations with nonrandom mating.
   d. Both (a) and (b)

_____ 5. In large, randomly mating populations, the frequencies of alleles and genotypes remain constant from generation to generation unless
   a. evolutionary forces are absent.
   b. evolutionary forces act on the population.
   c. the populations are *K*-strategists.
   d. the populations are *r*-strategists.

_____ 6. Natural selection acts on which of the following?
   a. genotypes   **c.** both phenotypes and genotypes
   b. phenotypes   **d.** neither phenotypes nor genotypes

_____ 7. Human height is an example of a
   a. single-gene trait.   **c.** monogenic trait.
   b. double-gene trait.   **d.** polygenic trait.

_____ 8. The range of phenotypes shifts toward one extreme in
   a. stabilizing selection.   **c.** directional selection.
   b. disruptive selection.   **d.** polygenic selection.

_____ 9. In a logistical model, exponential growth is limited by
   a. a density-independent factor.   **c.** a density-dependent factor.
   b. an unknown factor.   **d.** an exponential factor.

Test Prep Pretest *continued*

_____**10.** All of the individuals of a species that live together in one place at one
   time are
   a. *K*-strategists.
   b. a population.
   c. a density-dependent factor.
   d. *r*-strategists.

**In the space provided, write the letter of the description that best matches the
term or phrase.**

_____**11.** logistic

_____**12.** mutation

_____**13.** natural selection

_____**14.** *r*-strategists

_____**15.** stabilizing selection

a. short lifespans and many offspring

b. frequencies of the intermediate phenotypes
increase

c. a model of population growth that assumes
that birth rates and death rates vary with
population size

d. rates in nature are very slow

e. does not operate on rare, recessive alleles
that are not expressed

Complete each statement by writing the correct term or phrase in the space provided.

16. To predict how a population will grow, demographers construct a(n)

_____ of a population, a hypothetical population with the

key characteristics of the real population being studied.

17. Organisms that produce few offspring that mature slowly are called

_____ .

18. A female robin who chooses a male based on how well he sings is

demonstrating _____ _____ .

19. Migration to or from a population results in _____

_____ .

20. If the graph of the phenotypes of a trait in a population is a hill-shaped curve,

the trait exhibits a(n) _____ _____ .

21. When a recessive allele is present at a frequency of 0.1, only 1 out of 100

individuals will be homozygous recessive and will display the phenotype

associated with this allele. However, 18 out of 1,000 individuals will be

_____ and will carry the allele unexpressed.

Test Prep Pretest *continued*

Read each question, and write your answer in the space provided

22. Why does natural selection slowly reduce the frequency of harmful recessive alleles?

_____

_____

_____

_____

_____

_____

Questions 23 and 24 refer to the equations below.

$$\textbf{A. } \Delta N = rN$$

$$\textbf{B. } \Delta N = rN \frac{(K - N)}{K}$$

23. What number is being calculated in equation A?

_____

24. What happens when N approaches K in equation B?

_____

_____

Question 25 refers to the figures below.

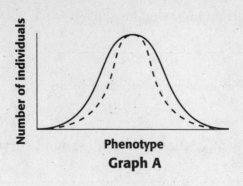

Graph A

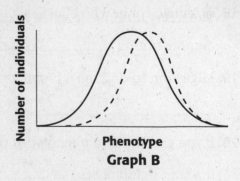

Graph B

25. What type of distribution does the solid-line curve in each of the graphs above represent?

_____

Skills Worksheet

Vocabulary Review

Complete each statement by writing the correct term or phrase from the list below in the space provided.

abiotic factors	ecology	primary succession
biodiversity	ecosystem	secondary succession
biotic factors	habitat	succession
community	pioneer species	

1. The number of species living within an ecosystem is a measure of its

_____ .

2. A somewhat regular progression of species replacement is called

_____ .

3. A(n) _____ consists of a community and all the physical aspects of its habitat, such as the soil, water, and weather.

4. The living organisms in a habitat are called _____

_____ .

5. The first organisms to live in a new habitat are small, fast-growing plants

called _____ _____ .

6. Succession that occurs where plants have not grown before is

called_____ _____ .

7. The many different species that live together in a habitat are called

a(n) _____ .

8. The study of the interactions of living organisms with one another and

with their environment is called _____ .

9. Succession that occurs where previous growth has occurred is called

_____ _____ .

10. The physical aspects of a habitat are called _____

_____ .

11. The place where a particular population of a species lives is called its

_____ .

In the space provided, write the letter of the description that best matches the term or phrase.

_____ **12.** primary productivity

_____ **13.** producers

_____ **14.** consumers

_____ **15.** trophic level

_____ **16.** food chain

_____ **17.** herbivore

_____ **18.** carnivore

_____ **19.** omnivore

_____ **20.** detritivore

_____ **21.** decomposers

_____ **22.** food web

_____ **23.** energy pyramid

_____ **24.** biomass

_____ **25.** biogeochemical cycle

_____ **26.** ground water

_____ **27.** transpiration

_____ **28.** nitrogen fixation

a. an interconnected group of food chains

b. a pathway formed when a substance enters a living organism, stays for a time in the organism, then returns to the nonliving environment

c. the dry weight of tissue and other organic matter found in a specific ecosystem

d. organisms in an ecosystem that first capture energy

e. water retained beneath the surface of Earth

f. the rate at which organic material is produced by photosynthetic organisms

g. a diagram in which each trophic level is represented by a block with a width proportional to the amount of energy stored in the organisms at that trophic level

h. the process of combining nitrogen with hydrogen to form ammonia

i. organisms that obtain energy by consuming plants or other organisms

j. the evaporation of water from the leaves of plants

k. a level in a diagram based on the organism's source of energy

l. an organism that obtains energy from organic wastes and dead bodies

m. the path of energy through the trophic levels of an ecosystem

n. bacteria and fungi that cause decay

o. an animal that is both a herbivore and a carnivore

p. an animal that eats other animals

q. an animal that eats plants or other primary producers

Skills Worksheet

Test Prep Pretest

In the space provided, write the letter of the term or phrase that best completes each statement or best answers each question.

_____ **1.** Biodiversity is the number of species
   a. of animals living within an ecosystem.
   b. of plants and fungi living within an ecosystem.
   c. of bacteria and protists living within an ecosystem.
   d. living within an ecosystem.

_____ **2.** The plants that first grow on an island formed by a volcano are part of a progression called
   a. primary succession.   **c.** secondary succession.
   b. primary productivity.   **d.** the climax community.

_____ **3.** In the living portion of the water cycle, water
   a. is retained beneath the surface of Earth as ground water.
   b. evaporates from the soil.
   c. evaporates from dead organisms.
   d. is taken up by the roots of plants.

Questions 4–7 refer to the figure at right.

_____ **4.** The algae are
   a. decomposers.
   b. consumers.
   c. producers.
   d. herbivores.

_____ **5.** The krill are
   a. decomposers.
   b. consumers.
   c. producers.
   d. detritivores.

_____ **6.** This figure is called a
   a. food chain.
   b. food web.
   c. pyramid of energy.
   d. trophic level.

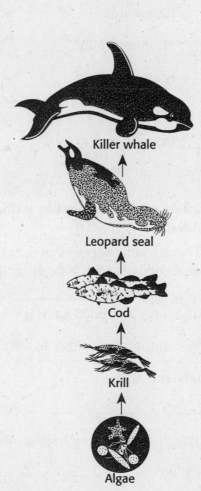

Killer whale

Leopard seal

Cod

Krill

Algae

_____ **7.** The most likely reason that this figure shows only five levels is that
   a. pollution probably destroyed all of the higher levels.
   b. no other organisms are powerful enough to kill and eat the killer whale.
   c. too much energy is lost at each level to permit more levels.
   d. there is not enough energy initially present at the first level.

_____ **8.** The process of succession varies depending on
   a. the plant species involved.
   b. initial environmental conditions and chance.
   c. pioneer species.
   d. competition between species.

_____ **9.** The conversion of nitrate to nitrogen gas is called
   a. assimilation.   **c.** nitrification.
   b. ammonification.   **d.** denitrification.

In the space provided, write the letter of the description that best matches the term or phrase.

_____ **10.** habitat

_____ **11.** community

_____ **12.** ecosystem

_____ **13.** herbivores

_____ **14.** carnivores

a. animals at the second trophic level that eat plants

b. the place where a particular population of a species lives

c. the many species that live together in a habitat

d. animals at the third trophic level that eat other animals

e. a community and all the physical aspects of its habitat

Complete each statement by writing the correct term or phrase in the space provided.

15. The physical aspects, or _____ _____ , of an ecosystem's habitat include soil, water, and weather.

16. In a(n) _____ _____ , the amount of energy stored at each level determines the width of each block.

17. The amount of energy in a trophic level is more accurately determined by

measuring the _____ (dry weight of tissue) than the

_____ of organisms.

18. The process of combining nitrogen gas with hydrogen to form ammonia is

called _____ _____ .

Test Prep Pretest *continued*

19. The production of ammonia by bacteria during the decay of nitrogen-

containing urea is called _____ .

Read each question, and write your answer in the space provided.

20. What components are included in an ecosystem but not in a community?

_____

_____

_____

21. Why are energy pyramids never inverted?

_____

_____

_____

22. Trace the cycling of water between the atmosphere and Earth.

_____

_____

_____

_____

23. List the four stages of the nitrogen cycle.

_____

_____

_____

| Test Prep Pretest *continued*

Questions 24 and 25 refer to the figure below, which shows the carbon cycle.

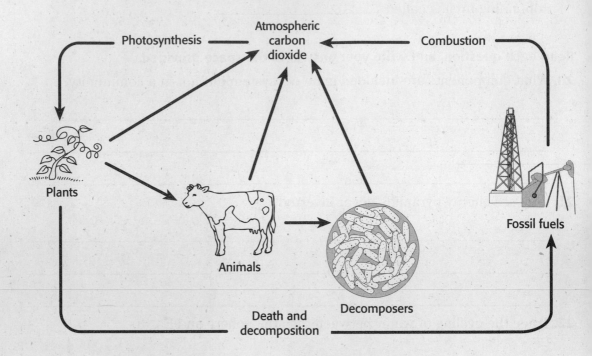

24. How do the living organisms in the figure return carbon atoms to the pool of carbon dioxide in the atmosphere and water?

_____

_____

_____

25. What is the source of the carbon in fossil fuels?

_____

_____

_____

Skills Worksheet

Vocabulary Review

In the space provided, write the letter of the description that best matches the term or phrase.

_____ **1.** coevolution

_____ **2.** predation

_____ **3.** parasitism

_____ **4.** secondary compound

_____ **5.** symbiosis

_____ **6.** mutualism

_____ **7.** commensalism

_____ **8.** competition

_____ **9.** niche

_____ **10.** fundamental niche

_____ **11.** realized niche

_____ **12.** competitive exclusion

_____ **13.** biodiversity

a. defensive chemical used by plants

b. a relationship in which both participating species benefit

c. the entire range of conditions an organism is potentially able to occupy

d. when two species use the same resource

e. back-and-forth evolutionary adjustments between interacting members of an ecosystem

f. two or more species living together in a close, long-term relationship

g. the fundamental role of a species in an ecosystem

h. one organism feeds on and usually lives on or in another larger organism

i. the elimination of a competing species

j. the part of its fundamental niche that a species occupies

k. a relationship in which one species benefits and the other is neither harmed nor helped

l. the variety of living organisms in a community

m. the act of one organism feeding on another

Complete each statement by writing the correct term or phrase in the space provided.

14. The prevailing weather conditions in any given area are called

the_____ .

15. A(n) _____ is a major biological community that occurs over a large area of land.

16. The _____ _____ is a shallow zone near the shore.

| Vocabulary Review *continued*

17. The _____ _____ is away from the shore but close to the surface.

18. The _____ _____ is a deep-water zone below the limits of effective light penetration.

19. Small organisms that drift in the upper waters of the ocean are called

_____ .

Skills Worksheet)

Test Prep Pretest

In the space provided, write the letter of the term or phrase that best completes each statement or best answers each question.

_____ 1. What form of interaction is taking place when a shark devours a seal?
  a. commensalism
  b. mutualism
  c. predation
  d. parasitism

_____ 2. When lions and hyenas fight over a dead zebra, their interaction is called
  a. mutualism.
  b. competition.
  c. commensalism.
  d. parasitism.

_____ 3. Mutualism and commensalism are two types of
  a. symbiosis.
  b. competition.
  c. parasitism.
  d. predation.

_____ 4. In the face of competition, an organism may occupy only part of its fundamental niche. That part is called its
  a. biome.
  b. community.
  c. realized niche.
  d. ecosystem.

_____ 5. Which of the following is NOT part of a freshwater habitat?
  a. profundal zone
  b. tidal zone
  c. littoral zone
  d. limnetic zone

_____ 6. The most important elements of climate are
  a. temperature and weather.
  b. temperature and moisture.
  c. moisture and sun.
  d. rainfall and snowfall.

_____ 7. The greater a community's biodiversity is, the greater is its
  a. productivity and stability.
  b. drought-tolerance.
  c. degree of competition.
  d. Both (a) and (b)

_____ 8. A major biological community that occurs over a large area of land is called a
  a. biome.
  b. profundal zone.
  c. niche.
  d. population.

_____ 9. Biomes characterized by high annual rainfalls are generally located at
  a. high elevations.
  b. low latitudes.
  c. high latitudes.
  d. Both (a) and (c)

_____ 10. Herds of grazing mammals are found in
  a. the taiga.
  b. the tropical forest.
  c. the savanna.
  d. the desert.

| Test Prep Pretest *continued*

Complete each statement by writing the correct term or phrase in the space provided.

11. A characteristic of _____ is that they often do not kill their prey because they depend on the prey for food, a place to live, and a means to transmit their offspring.

12. Virtually all plants contain defensive chemicals called _____

_____ .

13. Mild climate and annual precipitation of 75–250 cm favor the growth of the

type of biome called _____ _____

_____ .

14. The entire range of conditions an organism can tolerate is its

_____ _____ .

15. Back-and-forth evolutionary adjustments between interacting members of an

ecosystem are called _____ .

16. When sea stars were kept out of experimental plots in the coastal community

studied by Robert Paine, the number of species in the ecosystem

_____ .

17. Fewer than 25 cm of precipitation per year falls in two of the world's biomes—

the desert and the _____ .

18. Latitude is a measure of distance from the _____ .

19. A prairie is a biome called _____ _____ .

Read each question, and write your answer in the space provided.

20. Why is parasitism considered a special case of predation?

_____

_____

_____

_____

21. Explain how the larvae of the cabbage butterfly have overcome the mustard plant's defenses.

_____

_____

_____

_____

22. Explain how predation, competition, and biodiversity are related.

_____

_____

_____

_____

_____

_____

23. Explain how three species of warblers that consume insects in spruce trees can occupy the same forest without violating Gause's principle.

_____

_____

_____

_____

24. Where are the world's most abundant fishing grounds located? Explain.

_____

_____

_____

_____

| Test Prep Pretest *continued*

Question 25 refers to the figure below, which shows the results of Gause's experiments with paramecia.

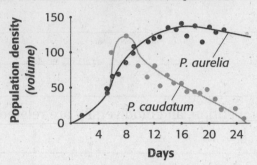

Effects of Competition

25. What principle does this graph illustrate?

_____

_____

Skills Worksheet
Vocabulary Review

Complete each statement by writing the correct term or phrase in the space provided.

1. When sulfur combines with water vapor to form sulfuric acid, the resulting precipitation is called _____ _____ .

2. The major cause of ozone destruction is a class of chemicals, invented in the 1920s, called _____ .

3. The warming of the atmosphere that results from greenhouse gases is known as the _____ _____ .

4. As molecules of chlorinated hydrocarbons pass up through the trophic levels of the food chain, they become increasingly concentrated. This process is called _____ _____ .

5. Porous rock reservoirs for ground water are called _____ .

In the space provided, write the letter of the description that best matches the term or phrase.

_____ **6.** global change

_____ **7.** ozone hole

_____ **8.** malignant melanoma

_____ **9.** greenhouse gases

_____ **10.** chlorinated hydrocarbons

_____ **11.** carcinogen

a. a class of compounds that includes DDT, chlordane, lindane, and dieldrin

b. examples include acid rain and ozone destruction

c. a zone in the atmosphere with a below-normal concentration of ozone

d. a potentially lethal form of skin cancer

e. a cancer-causing agent

f. gases with insulating effects

Name _____ Class _____ Date _____

Test Prep Pretest

In the space provided, write the letter of the term or phrase that best completes each statement or best answers each question.

_____ 1. When the sulfur in the atmosphere combines with water vapor, the result is
  a. ozone.
  b. CFCs.
  c. acid rain.
  d. ultraviolet radiation.

_____ 2. Global levels of carbon dioxide are
  a. rising.
  b. remaining constant.
  c. falling.
  d. too low to be measured accurately.

_____ 3. All of the following are considered nonreplaceable resources EXCEPT
  a. topsoil.
  b. wood.
  c. ground water.
  d. animal and plant species.

_____ 4. If current birth rates and death rates remain constant, the world's population will double in
  a. 20 years.
  b. 30 years.
  c. 40 years.
  d. 60 years.

_____ 5. In which of the following countries is population growth most rapid?
  a. United States
  b. Nigeria
  c. Australia
  d. Japan

_____ 6. Worldwide efforts to reduce pollution include all of the following EXCEPT
  a. severe restrictions on the use of DDT.
  b. taxation and legislation.
  c. international agreements to stop CFC production.
  d. an international agreement to close all coal-burning facilities.

_____ 7. The first stage of addressing an environmental problem is
  a. assessment.
  b. risk analysis.
  c. public education.
  d. political action.

Test Prep Pretest *continued*

Complete each statement by writing the correct term or phrase in the space provided.

8. Because of the current condition of the ozone layer, more

_____ _____ is reaching Earth's

surface.

9. The insulating effect of various gases in Earth's atmosphere is known as the

_____ _____ .

10. The increase in global temperatures is called _____

_____ .

11. Examples of chemical pollutants released into the global ecosystem by the

agriculture industry are _____ _____ ,

and _____ .

12. Since 1650, the human _____ _____

has remained constant, and the _____

_____ has fallen steadily.

13. In the United States, the population _____

_____ is less than half the global rate.

14. Washing cars and watering lawns less often and using efficient faucets are

ways to conserve _____ _____ .

15. The Clean Air Act of 1990 requires that power plants install

_____ on their smokestacks.

Read each question, and write your answer in the space provided.

16. How does the presence of the ozone layer affect life on Earth?

_____

_____

_____

17. Explain the relationship between the greenhouse effect and global warming.

_____

_____

_____

_____

_____

18. Explain biological magnification.

_____

_____

_____

_____

19. What has happened to the human death rate in the past several hundred years? Explain.

_____

_____

_____

_____

20. List the five components necessary to solve an environmental problem successfully.

_____

_____

Vocabulary Review

In the space provided, write the letter of the description that best matches the term or phrase.

_____ **1.** colonial organism

_____ **2.** aggregation

_____ **3.** multicellular organism

_____ **4.** differentiation

_____ **5.** protists

_____ **6.** hypha

_____ **7.** tissue

_____ **8.** organ

_____ **9.** organ system

_____**10.** vascular tissue

_____**11.** invertebrates

_____**12.** vertebrates

a. animals that have a backbone

b. a group of specialized cells that transport water and dissolved nutrients

c. a collection of organs that carry out a major body function

d. animals that lack a backbone

e. distinct group of cells with a similar structure and function

f. a group of cells that are permanently associated but do not communicate with one another

g. a strand of connected fungal cells

h. the process by which cells become specialized in form and function

i. an organism composed of many cells that are permanently associated with one another and that coordinate their activities

j. a collection of cells that come together for a period of time and then separate

k. tissues organized into a specialized structure with a specific function

l. eukaryotes that are not fungi, plants, or animals

Skills Worksheet

Test Prep Pretest

In the space provided, write the letter of the term or phrase that best completes each statement or best answers each question.

_____ 1. A collection of cells that come together for a period of time and then separate is called
    a. a colony.
    b. an aggregation.
    c. multicellular.
    d. a tissue.

_____ 2. Which of the following statements about protists is NOT true?
    a. Protists are eukaryotes that are neither fungi, plants, nor animals.
    b. Some protists use flagella to move.
    c. All single-celled prokaryotes are protists.
    d. Many protists reproduce sexually and asexually.

_____ 3. The bodies of fungi consist of long strands of connected cells called
    a. septa.
    b. spores.
    c. cilia.
    d. hyphae.

_____ 4. Most animals and plants have groups of cells with a similar structure and function that are organized into
    a. organ systems.
    b. tissues.
    c. nerves and muscles.
    d. All of the above

_____ 5. Plant cells have cell walls composed of which of the following?
    a. cellulose
    b. chitin
    c. silica
    d. peptidoglycan

_____ 6. A type of plant tissue that transports water and dissolved nutrients is called
    a. vascular tissue.
    b. spongy tissue.
    c. nerve tissue.
    d. muscle tissue.

Complete each statement by writing the correct term or phrase in the space provided.

7. The two kingdoms in which all members are heterotrophs are

_____ and _____ .

8. One distinguishing characteristic of bacteria is the _____

_____ sequences of the ribosome proteins and RNA

polymerases.

9. Eukaryotes and archaebacteria have genes that are interrupted by

_____ .

10. Cells of the plasmodial slime mold come together temporarily to form

a(n) _____ , whereas the cells of *Volvox* are permanently

associated as a(n) _____ _____ .

11. The only domain that includes multicellular organisms is

_____ .

12. The kind of protist responsible for the disease malaria is called a(n)

_____ .

13. Fungi that make mushrooms belong to the phylum _____ .

14. Animal cells differ from plant cells in that animal cells have no

_____ _____ .

Read each question, and write your answer in the space provided.

15. List the six kingdoms, and indicate whether the organisms in each kingdom
are prokaryotic or eukaryotic.

_____

_____

_____

_____

16. How do nonvascular plants differ from vascular plants? Give an example
of each.

_____

_____

_____

_____

_____

Test Prep Pretest *continued*

Questions 17–19 refer to the figure at right, which shows a phylogenetic tree of the six kingdoms.

17. Explain why the kingdom Archaebacteria is located on the branch of the tree that leads to the kingdoms Protista, Animalia, Plantae, and Fungi.

_____

_____

_____

_____

_____

_____

_____

18. Does the phylogenetic tree separate prokaryotes from eukaryotes? Explain.

_____

_____

_____

19. Explain why splitting archaebacteria and eubacteria into two separate kingdoms is justified.

_____

_____

_____

_____

_____

_____

20. List the six categories of animals, and give an example of each.

_____

_____

_____

_____

_____

_____

Name _____ Class _____ Date _____

Vocabulary Review

Use the terms from the list below to fill in the blanks in the following passage.

bacteriophages	glycoproteins	prions
capsid	lysogenic cycle	provirus
emerging viruses	lytic cycle	viroids
envelope	pathogen	viruses

Segments of nucleic acids contained in a protein coat are called

(1) _____ . The protein coat, or **(2)** _____ ,

may contain RNA or DNA, but not both. Many viruses have a(n)

(3) _____ , which surrounds the capsid and helps the virus

enter cells. It consists of proteins, lipids, and **(4)** _____ derived

from the host cell. Viruses that infect bacteria are called

(5) _____ .

Any agent that causes disease is called a(n) **(6)** _____ .

Viruses cause damage when they replicate inside cells many times. When the

viruses break out, the cell is destroyed. The cycle of infection, replication, and

cell destruction is called the **(7)** _____

_____ .

During an infection, some viruses stay inside the cells but do not make new

viruses. Instead, the viral gene is inserted into the host chromosome and is called

a(n) **(8)** _____ . Whenever the cell divides, the provirus also

divides, resulting in two infected host cells. This type of replication cycle is called

a(n) **(9)** _____ _____ .

Viruses that evolve in a geographically isolated area and are pathogenic to

humans are called **(10)** _____ _____ .

Infectious disease agents that have a single strand of RNA and have no capsid

are called **(11)** _____ .

| Vocabulary Review *continued*

There is a newly discovered class of infectious particles called

(12) _____ , which are composed of protein with

no nucleic acid.

In the space provided, write the letter of the description that best matches the term or phrase.

_____**13.** pilus

_____**14.** bacillus

_____**15.** coccus

_____**16.** spirillum

_____**17.** capsule

_____**18.** antibiotics

_____**19.** endospores

_____**20.** conjugation

_____**21.** anaerobic

_____**22.** aerobic

_____**23.** toxins

a. a gel-like layer outside the cell wall and membrane

b. spiral-shaped bacterium

c. bacterial structures that can survive environmental stress

d. an outgrowth on bacteria that attaches to surfaces or other cells

e. round-shaped bacterium

f. a process in which two organisms exchange genetic material

g. oxygen-free environment

h. environment with oxygen

i. chemicals poisonous to eukaryotic cells

j. rod-shaped bacterium

k. chemicals that interfere with life processes in bacteria

Name _____ Class _____ Date _____

Test Prep Pretest

In the space provided, write the letter of the description that best matches the term or phrase.

_____ 1. capsid

_____ 2. envelope

_____ 3. glycoproteins

_____ 4. bacteriophage

_____ 5. pathogen

_____ 6. lytic cycle

_____ 7. provirus

_____ 8. lysogenic cycle

_____ 9. bacillus

_____ 10. coccus

_____ 11. spirillum

_____ 12. antibiotic

_____ 13. heterotrophic bacteria

a. a host chromosome with a viral gene inserted into it

b. proteins with carbohydrate molecules attached

c. a drug that interferes with the life processes in bacteria

d. a rod-shaped bacterial cell

e. bacteria that feed on organic material formed by other organisms

f. a spiral-shaped bacterial cell

g. a virus's protein coat

h. a cycle in which the viral genome replicates without destroying the host cell

i. a bacteria-infecting virus

j. a cycle of viral infection, replication, and cell destruction

k. a round bacterial cell

l. an agent that causes disease

m. surrounds the capsid of many viruses and helps them enter cells

Complete each statement by writing the correct term or phrase in the space provided.

14. A(n) _____ is a segment of nucleic acids contained in a protein coat.

15. Viruses must rely on _____ _____ for replication.

16. The capsid of viruses may enclose either the nucleic acid

_____ or the nucleic acid _____ .

17. Infectious particles called _____ are composed of proteins and have no nucleic acid.

18. HIV gradually infects and destroys so many _____ cells that people with AIDS often die of infections that a healthy immune system would normally resist.

19. The _____ of *E. coli* have two main functions: to adhere to surfaces and to join bacterial cells prior to conjugation.

20. In the presence of hydrogen-rich chemicals, _____ bacteria can manufacture all of their own amino acids and proteins.

Questions 21 and 22 refer to the figure below, which shows the human immunodeficiency virus (HIV).

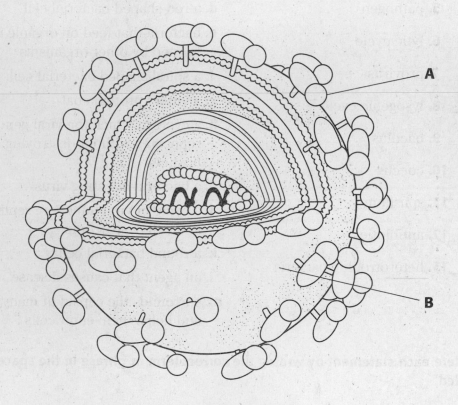

21. The structure labeled *A* is derived from the membrane of the

_____ _____ .

22. The structure labeled *B* is a(n) _____ .

Name _____ Class _____ Date _____

Read each question, and write your answer in the space provided.

23. Describe how HIV reproduces.

_____

_____

_____

_____

24. How does *E. coli* reproduce?

_____

_____

25. How was the tobacco mosaic virus discovered?

_____

_____

_____

_____

_____

_____

Name _____ Class _____ Date _____

Vocabulary Review

Complete the crossword puzzle using the clues provided.

ACROSS

1. a protist that lives in the guts of termites
3. _____ of generations: a life cycle characterized by a sporophyte phase and a gametophyte phase
4. a photosynthetic protist
6. a flexible, cytoplasmic extension
8. a diploid zygote with a thick protective wall
11. the stage of life cycle of *Plasmodium* that infects red blood cells
12. the stage of life cycle of *Plasmodium* that infects the liver

13. has double shell
14. short flagellum used for movement

ACROSS

2. a reproductive cell that produces haploid spores by meiosis
5. protists with no cell walls or flagella
7. a freshwater protist with two flagella
9. a mass of cytoplasm that looks like oozing slime
10. a heterotrophic protist

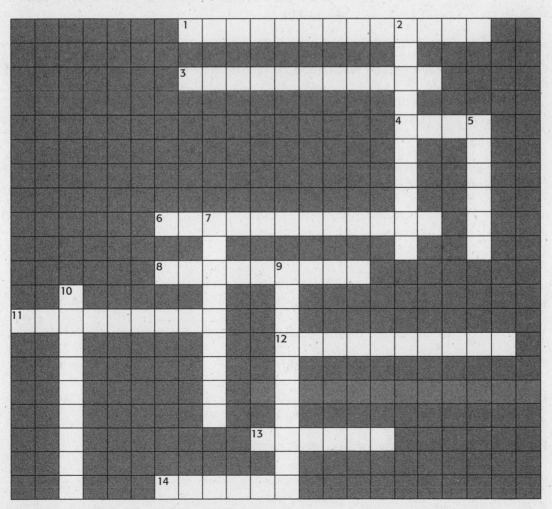

Test Prep Pretest

In the space provided, write the letter of the description that best matches the term or phrase.

_____ **1.** green algae

_____ **2.** red algae

_____ **3.** brown algae

_____ **4.** zygospore

_____ **5.** cellular slime molds

_____ **6.** diatoms

a. a diploid zygote in *Chlamydomonas* with a thick, protective wall

b. individual organisms that behave as separate amoebas; gather together to form slugs during times of environmental stress

c. most are freshwater, unicellular organisms; some are large, multicellular marine organisms

d. multicellular; found mostly in marine environments

e. multicellular organisms found in warm ocean waters; their color results from red photosynthetic pigments

f. photosynthetic unicellular protists with double shells

Complete each statement by writing the correct term or phrase in the space provided.

7. Two of the most important features that evolved among the protists are

_____ _____ and _____ .

8. Some protists have _____ , small organelles containing light-sensitive pigments that detect changes in the quality and intensity of light.

9. During conjugation, protists exchange _____

_____ .

10. *Ulva* is characterized by two distinct multicellular phases: a diploid, spore-producing phase called the _____ generation and a haploid, gamete-producing phase called the _____ generation.

11. Long, thin projections of _____ extend through the pores in a foram's test to aid in swimming and in catching prey.

12. Diatoms can have one of two types of symmetry, which are

_____ or _____ .

Test Prep Pretest *continued*

13. The large brown algae that grow along coasts are known as

_____ .

14. The stage of *Plasmodium* that lives in mosquitoes and is injected into humans

is called the _____ ; the second stage of the *Plasmodium*

life cycle is called the _____ .

Questions 15–17 refer to the figure at right, which shows a paramecium.

15. The structures labeled *A* are

_____ , which enable the
paramecium to move through the water.

16. The structure labeled *B* is a(n)

_____ _____ .

17. The structure labeled *C* is a(n)

_____ _____ .

Read each question, and write your answer in the space provided.

18. What diseases caused by protists can be transmitted to humans through drinking water?

_____

_____

19. In what three environments are protists found?

_____

_____

20. Compare the reproductive cycle of *Ulva* with the reproductive cycle of *Spirogyra*. What kinds of protists are *Ulva* and *Spirogyra*?

_____

_____

Test Prep Pretest *continued*

21. List three of the different types of sexual reproduction in protists.

_____

_____

_____

22. What groups of protists use extensions of cytoplasm for locomotion?

_____

23. What are diatoms, and how are they beneficial?

_____

_____

_____

_____

_____

24. How do diatoms move around?

_____

_____

25. How do people become infected with malaria?

_____

_____

_____

_____

Vocabulary Review

In the space provided, write the letter of the description that best matches the term or phrase.

_____ 1. chitin

_____ 2. hyphae

_____ 3. mycelium

_____ 4. zygosporangium

_____ 5. stolon

_____ 6. rhizoid

_____ 7. ascus

_____ 8. yeasts

_____ 9. budding

_____ 10. basidium

_____ 11. mycorrhizae

_____ 12. lichen

a. a type of mutualistic relationship formed between fungi and the roots of vascular plants

b. a thick-walled sexual structure

c. the tough polysaccharide found in the hard outer covering of insects and fungal cell walls

d. a symbiosis between a fungus and a photosynthetic partner

e. the hyphae that anchor a fungus to its source of food

f. slender filaments that compose the body of a fungus

g. tangled mass formed by hyphae

h. the mycelia that grow along the surface of a fungus's food

i. a saclike structure in which haploid spores are formed

j. the common name given to unicellular ascomycetes

k. a club-shaped sexual reproductive structure

l. asexual reproduction in which a small cell forms from a larger cell by pinching itself off from the larger cell

Name _____ Class _____ Date _____

Test Prep Pretest

In the space provided, write the letter of the term or phrase that best completes each statement or best answers each question.

_____ 1. Which of the following is NOT a characteristic of fungi?
　　a. filamentous bodies　　　　**c.** chlorophyll
　　b. cell walls made of chitin　**d.** nuclear mitosis

_____ 2. A mycelium helps a fungus absorb nutrients from its environment because it provides
　　a. minerals.
　　b. a high surface area-to-volume ratio.
　　c. digestive enzymes.
　　d. a low surface area-to-volume ratio.

Questions 3 and 4 refer to the figure at right.

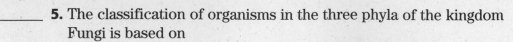

_____ 3. The fungus shown is a(n)
　　a. asomycete.
　　b. basidiomycete.
　　c. deuteromycete.
　　d. zygomycete.

_____ 4. The structure labeled *A* in the figure is called a
　　a. rhizoid.
　　b. spore.
　　c. stolon.
　　d. hypha.

_____ 5. The classification of organisms in the three phyla of the kingdom Fungi is based on
　　a. food.　　　　　　　　**c.** cellular structure.
　　b. digestive structures.　**d.** sexual reproductive structures.

_____ 6. Most fungal spores are formed by
　　a. the fusing of hyphae.　**c.** mitosis.
　　b. the fusing of asci.　　 **d.** None of the above

Complete each statement by underlining the correct term or phrase in the brackets.

7. The tough material found in the cell walls of all fungi is [cellulose / chitin].

8. The slender filaments that make up the bodies of most fungi are called [hyphae / mycelium].

9. In bread mold, the mycelia that grow along the surface of the bread are called [stolons / rhizoids].

10. During succession, [mycorrhizae / lichens] are often the first living organisms to appear in a new area.

11. In lichens, the algal partner provides [minerals / carbohydrates].

Complete each statement by writing the correct term or phrase in the space provided.

12. When you look at a lichen, you are looking at the _____ ,

which is usually a(n) _____ .

13. Fungi secrete _____ _____ that break down organic matter so they can then absorb the decomposed molecules.

14. Sexual reproduction in fungi is initiated when two _____ of opposite mating types fuse and form a reproductive structure.

15. The three phyla of fungi form distinctive structures during sexual reproduction.

Members of the phylum Zygomycota form _____ ;

members of the phylum Ascomycota form _____ ; and

members of the phylum Basidiomycota form _____ .

16. Fungi _____ nonliving organic matter and thus are

resource recyclers.

17. Certain fungi play important roles in the nutrition of vascular plants by form-

ing symbiotic associations with their roots, called _____ .

18. The underside of a mushroom cap is lined with rows of

_____ , which contain thousands of club-shaped structures

called _____ .

19. Fungi that are _____ compete for nutrients with their
hosts.

20. Fungi called _____ are commercially useful in baking,
brewing, and wine-making.

Read each question, and write your answer in the space provided.

21. Give four reasons fungi are no longer classified in the same kingdom as plants.

_____

_____

_____

_____

22. Distinguish between mitosis in fungi and mitosis in plants and most other eukaryotes.

_____

_____

_____

_____

_____

23. Why can lichen survive in habitats as diverse as polar and desert regions?

_____

_____

_____

_____

24. Give at least two examples of a beneficial and a harmful ascomycete.

_____

_____

_____

_____

25. Describe how _Amanita muscaria_ obtains nutrients.

_____

_____

_____

_____

Skills Worksheet

Vocabulary Review

In the space provided, write the letter of the description that best matches the term or phrase.

_____ 1. cuticle

_____ 2. embryo

_____ 3. flower

_____ 4. guard cell

_____ 5. meristem

_____ 6. nonvascular plant

_____ 7. phloem

_____ 8. root

_____ 9. seed

_____ 10. seed plant

_____ 11. shoot

_____ 12. stoma

_____ 13. vascular plant

_____ 14. vascular system

_____ 15. xylem

a. a waxy layer that covers the nonwoody aboveground parts of most plants

b. permits plants to exchange oxygen and carbon dioxide

c. one of a pair of specialized cells that open and close the stomata

d. a system of well-developed vascular tissues

e. a plant that has no vascular system

f. a plant with a vascular system

g. a structure that contains a plant embryo

h. a vascular plant that produces seeds

i. a reproductive structure that produces pollen and seeds

j. tissue made of soft-walled cells that transport organic nutrients

k. tissue made of hard-walled cells that transport water and mineral nutrients

l. the part of a plant's body that grows mostly upward

m. the part of a plant's body that grows mostly downward

n. zone of actively dividing plant cells

o. an early stage in the development of a plant or an animal

Vocabulary Review *continued*

In the space provided, explain how the terms in each pair differ in meaning.

16. rhizoid, rhizome

_____

_____

_____

17. frond, cone

_____

_____

_____

18. gymnosperm, angiosperm

_____

_____

_____

19. fruit, endosperm

_____

_____

_____

20. monocot, dicot

_____

_____

_____

21. vegetative part, vegetable

_____

_____

_____

22. cereal, grain

_____

_____

_____

Test Prep Pretest

Questions 1–4 refer to the figure below, which shows the life cycle of a plant.

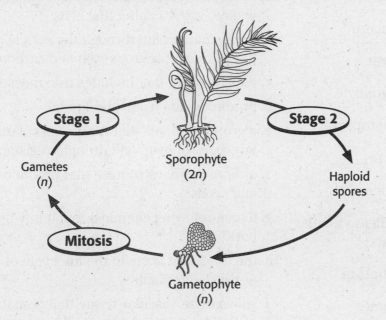

_____ 1. What process occurs at stage 1?
   a. mitosis
   b. meiosis
   c. fertilization
   d. cell division

_____ 2. The structures produced by stage 1 are
   a. spore capsules.
   b. diploid spores.
   c. haploid spores.
   d. zygotes.

_____ 3. What process occurs at stage 2?
   a. fertilization
   b. pollination
   c. meiosis
   d. mitosis

_____ 4. The life cycle above is called
   a. a haploid life cycle.
   b. alternation of generations.
   c. a diploid life cycle.
   d. an incomplete life cycle.

In the space provided, write the letter of the description that best matches the term or phrase.

_____ **5.** rayon

_____ **6.** stomata

_____ **7.** flower

_____ **8.** sporophyte

_____ **9.** gametophyte

_____ **10.** xylem

_____ **11.** phloem

_____ **12.** seedless vascular plants

_____ **13.** Bryophyta

_____ **14.** legumes

_____ **15.** grain

_____ **16.** salicin

a. sporophyte vascular tissue that contains hard-walled, water-conducting cells

b. pores that extend through the cuticle and permit plants to exchange oxygen and carbon dioxide

c. plant phylum that includes true mosses

d. product made from wood pulp

e. a group of plants that have a vascular system, a large sporophyte, and drought-resistant spores

f. a reproductive structure that produces pollen and seeds

g. a pain-relieving chemical found in willow tree bark

h. the dominant stage in the life cycle of nonvascular plants

i. sporophyte vascular tissue that contains soft-walled, sugar-conducting cells

j. the dominant stage in the life cycle of vascular plants

k. plants of the pea family that produce protein-rich seeds in long pods

l. edible dry fruit of a cereal grass

Complete each statement by writing the correct term or phrase in the space provided.

17. When specialized cells called _____

_____ change shape, stomata open and close.

18. The part of a plant's body that grows mostly upward is called the

_____ ; the part that grows downward is called the

_____ .

19. In nonvascular plants, the smaller, nongreen _____

generation depends on the _____ generation for nutrients.

20. Seed plants whose seeds do not develop within a fruit are called

_____ .

21. Plants in phylum Pterophyta have coiled young leaves called

_____ and _____ that produce

spores on the lower side of fronds.

22. Botanically, a(n) _____ is the part of a plant that contains

seeds, and a(n) _____ _____ is any

nonreproductive part of a plant.

Read each question, and write your answer in the space provided.

23. Describe the fundamental differences between vascular and nonvascular
plants.

_____

_____

_____

_____

_____

_____

24. List four ways that seeds have influenced the evolution of plants on land.

_____

_____

_____

_____

_____

25. Describe the two types of angiosperms, and list two examples of each.

_____

_____

_____

_____

_____

Skills Worksheet

Vocabulary Review

In the space provided, write the letter of the description that best matches the term or phrase.

_____ **1.** a structure in seedless plants that produces eggs

_____ **2.** a structure in seedless plants that produces sperm

_____ **3.** a cluster of sporangia on a fern frond

_____ **4.** contains a male gametophyte of a seed plant

_____ **5.** the part of the sporophyte in which the female gametophyte develops

_____ **6.** the transfer of pollen grains from the male to the female reproductive structure

_____ **7.** grows from a pollen grain to an ovule

_____ **8.** protects the embryo of a seed from mechanical injury

_____ **9.** leaflike structure that is part of a plant embryo

_____ **10.** one of the flower parts that protects a flower from damage when it is a bud

_____ **11.** one of the flower parts that attract pollinators

_____ **12.** a flower structure that consists of a threadlike filament topped with an anther

_____ **13.** a pollen-producing sac

_____ **14.** female reproductive part of a flower, consisting of an ovary, style, and stigma

_____ **15.** a pistil's swollen lower portion

_____ **16.** two sperm fusing with cells of the female gametophyte to produce both a zygote and an endosperm

a. anther

b. antheridium

c. archegonium

d. cotyledon

e. double fertilization

f. ovary

g. ovule

h. petal

i. pistil

j. pollination

k. pollen grain

l. pollen tube

m. seed coat

n. sepal

o. sorus

p. stamen

Vocabulary Review *continued*

Complete each statement by writing the correct term or phrase in the space provided.

17. The type of reproduction by which plants produce offspring from vegetative

    parts is called _____ _____ .

18. Growing new plants from seeds or from vegetative parts is called

    _____ _____ .

19. In a technique called _____ _____ ,
    pieces of plant tissue are placed on a sterile medium and are used to grow
    plants.

Skills Worksheet

Test Prep Pretest

In the space provided, write the letter of the term or phrase that best completes each statement or best answers each question.

_____ 1. The gametophyte of a nonvascular plant produces sperm in a structure called a(n)
   a. sporangium.　　　　　　**c.** antheridium.
   b. archegonium.　　　　　　**d.** sorus.

_____ 2. In seedless vascular plants, the archegonia and antheridia develop on which of the following?
   a. roots of the gametophytes
   b. upper surfaces of the gametophytes
   c. lower surfaces of the sporophytes
   d. lower surfaces of the gametophytes

_____ 3. The purpose of cotyledons is to transfer nutrients to the
   a. embryo.　　　　　　　　**c.** gametophytes.
   b. leaves.　　　　　　　　　**d.** endosperm.

_____ 4. In gymnosperms, the female cones produce
   a. ovules.　　　　　　　　　**c.** ovules and seeds.
   b. pollen.　　　　　　　　　**d.** pollen and seeds.

_____ 5. The process by which two sperm fuse with cells of the female gametophyte to produce both a zygote and endosperm is called
   a. alternation of generations.
   b. meiosis.
   c. double fertilization.
   d. asexual reproduction.

_____ 6. The male reproductive parts of a flower are called
   a. petals.　　　　　　　　　**c.** sepals.
   b. stamens.　　　　　　　　**d.** pistils.

_____ 7. Kalanchoës reproduce sexually by
   a. stem cuttings.
   b. plantlets.
   c. tiny seeds produced in flowers.
   d. air roots.

_____ 8. Growing African violets from the leaf cuttings of a parent plant is one example of which of the following?
   a. plant propagation
   b. grafting
   c. sexual reproduction
   d. tissue culture

Name _____ Class _____ Date _____

In the space provided, write the letter of the description that best matches the term or phrase.

_____ **9.** pollination

_____ **10.** pollen grain

_____ **11.** seed coat

_____ **12.** sepals

_____ **13.** anther

_____ **14.** pistil

_____ **15.** bulb

a. the innermost whorl of a flower; produces ovules

b. forms from the hardened outer cell layers of an ovule

c. a type of modified stem with fleshy leaves

d. a pollen-producing sac at the top of a stamen

e. the outermost whorl of a flower

f. the male gametophyte of a seed plant

g. the transfer of pollen grains from a male reproductive structure of a plant to a female reproductive structure of a plant

Complete each statement by writing the correct term or phrase in the space provided.

16. Spores are produced in a(n) _____ in mosses. A cluster of these forms a(n) _____ in ferns.

17. In seed plants, male gametophytes develop into _____

_____ , and female gametophytes develop within the

_____ .

18. In both mosses and ferns, gametophytes produce female gametes inside

_____ and male gametes inside _____ .

19. In angiosperm flowers, gametophytes grow from haploid

_____ produced by meiosis within the

_____ , which produce ovules, and the

_____ , which produce pollen.

20. Ferns, irises, and sugarcane have modified stems called

_____ , which are used in _____

reproduction.

21. In angiosperms, a sperm cell fuses with two other haploid cells to form a(n)

_____ cell that develops into _____ .

Test Prep Pretest *continued*

Read each question, and write your answer in the space provided.

22. How are the life cycles of a moss and a fern similar? How are they different?

_____

_____

_____

_____

_____

_____

_____

Questions 23–25 refer to the figure below, which shows a fern life cycle.

23. What generation of the fern is labeled *A*?

_____

24. What is the name of the plant structure labeled *B*?

_____

25. What generation of the fern is labeled *C*?

_____

Skills Worksheet

Vocabulary Review

In the space provided, write the letter of the description that best matches the term or phrase.

_____ 1. epidermis

_____ 2. cork

_____ 3. vessels

_____ 4. sieve tube

_____ 5. cortex

_____ 6. root hair

_____ 7. root cap

_____ 8. herbaceous plant

_____ 9. vascular bundle

_____ 10. pith

_____ 11. heartwood

_____ 12. sapwood

_____ 13. petiole

_____ 14. mesophyll

a. a plant with stems that are flexible and usually green

b. ground tissue surrounding the vascular tissue in a root

c. conducting strands in xylem

d. the wood in the center of a mature stem or tree trunk

e. a stalk that attaches a leaf to a stem

f. one of the slender projections of epidermal cells just behind a root tip

g. the ground tissue in a leaf

h. a bundle of xylem and phloem in vascular plants

i. lies outside the heartwood and contains vessel cells that can conduct water

j. dermal tissue in the nonwoody parts of a plant

k. a conducting strand in phloem

l. dermal tissue on woody stems and roots

m. a cell mass that covers and protects an actively growing root tip

n. ground tissue in the center of a stem or root

Vocabulary Review *continued*

Complete each statement by writing the correct term or phrase in the space provided.

15. A type of tissue called _____ tissue forms the protective outer layer of a plant.

16. A type of tissue called _____ tissue makes up much of the inside of the nonwoody parts of a plant.

17. The loss of water vapor from a plant is called _____ .

18. The term _____ refers to a part of a plant that provides organic compounds for other parts of the plant.

19. The term _____ refers to a part of a plant that organic compounds are delivered to.

20. The movement of organic compounds within a plant from a source to a sink

is called _____ .

Name _____ Class _____ Date _____

Test Prep Pretest

In the space provided, write the letter of the term or phrase that best completes each statement or best answers each question.

_____ 1. What type of tissue forms the protective outer layers of the plant?
  a. ground   **c.** dermal
  b. xylem   **d.** phloem

_____ 2. The primary photosynthetic organs of plants are the
  a. leaves.   **c.** roots.
  b. stems.   **d.** flowers.

_____ 3. The vascular tissue of a leaf is found in the
  a. petiole.   **c.** mesophyll.
  b. veins.   **d.** palisade layer.

_____ 4. When stomata are open, water vapor diffuses out of a leaf in a process called
  a. photosynthesis.   **c.** osmosis.
  b. germination.   **d.** transpiration.

_____ 5. Water will keep moving upward in a plant as long as there is an unbroken column of water in the
  a. phloem.   **c.** roots.
  b. xylem.   **d.** stomata.

In the space provided, write the letter of the description that best matches the term or phrase.

_____ 6. dermal tissue

_____ 7. tracheids

_____ 8. petiole

_____ 9. palisade layer

_____ 10. node

_____ 11. pith

_____ 12. vascular bundle

_____ 13. cork

_____ 14. root hairs

a. slender projections from the epidermal cells just behind a root tip that increase the absorption of water and minerals

b. the inner layers of ground tissue in a stem

c. makes up the protective outer layer of a plant

d. a stalk that attaches a leaf to a stem

e. cluster of vascular tissues in a herbaceous stem

f. the dermal tissue on woody stems and roots; consists of several layers of dead cells

g. the point at which a leaf is attached to a stem

h. narrow, elongated xylem cells with pits through which water flows

i. rows of closely packed, columnar mesophyll cells just beneath the upper epidermis

Test Prep Pretest *continued*

Complete each statement by writing the correct term or phrase in the space provided.

15. The loss of water vapor by _____ creates a pull that

   draws water up through the vascular tissue called _____
   in the stem and into the leaves.

16. Roots take in water from the soil by the process called

   _____ .

17. The cells that carry out metabolic functions for the sieve-tube cells of phloem

   are called _____ _____ .

18. The _____ inside a sugar maple can be collected and
   refined for use in the production of maple syrup.

19. Dermal tissue prevents water loss, and it also functions in

   _____ exchange and the absorption of

   _____ _____ .

20. Ground tissue stores water, _____ , and

   _____ , and it contains and supports a plant's

   _____ tissue.

Read each question, and write your answer in the space provided.

21. Differentiate between nonwoody stems and woody stems.

   _____

   _____

   _____

   _____

   _____

   _____

22. How are the seeds of a sugar maple tree dispersed?

   _____

   _____

| Test Prep Pretest *continued*

23. Trace the movement of water through a plant.

_____

_____

_____

_____

Questions 24 and 25 refer to the figure below, which shows the pressure-flow model.

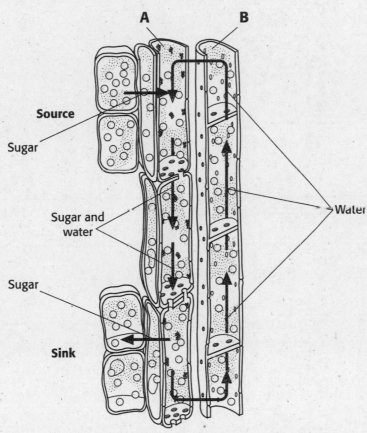

24. Identify the structure labeled *A*. What process enables sugar to enter this structure?

_____

_____

25. Identify the structure labeled *B*. What process enables water to leave this structure?

_____

_____

Skills Worksheet

Vocabulary Review

Write the correct term from the list below in the space next to its definition.

annual	cork cambium	primary growth
annual ring	germination	secondary growth
apical meristem	perennial	vascular cambium
biennial		

_____ **1.** a plant that lives for several years

_____ **2.** growth that increases the length or height of a plant

_____ **3.** the meristem that lies within the bark

_____ **4.** region where primary growth is produced

_____ **5.** plant that takes two growing seasons to complete its life cycle

_____ **6.** the meristem that lies just under the bark

_____ **7.** layer of secondary xylem formed each year

_____ **8.** a plant that completes its life cycle and dies within one growing season

_____ **9.** growth that increases the width of a plant's stems and roots

_____ **10.** when a plant embryo resumes its growth

In the space provided, write the letter of the description that best matches the term or phrase.

_____**11.** mineral nutrient

_____**12.** auxin

_____**13.** hormone

_____**14.** apical dominance

_____**15.** tropism

_____**16.** photoperiodism

_____**17.** dormancy

a. a response in which a plant grows either toward or away from a stimulus

b. condition in an inactive seed or plant

c. the inhibition of the growth of buds along a stem by the apical meristem

d. the response of plants to the length of days and nights

e. a chemical that causes a stem to bend toward light

f. needed by plants in small amounts

g. a chemical produced in one part of an organism and transported to another part, where it causes a response

Skills Worksheet

Test Prep Pretest

In the space provided, write the letter of the term or phrase that best completes each statement or best answers each question.

_____ 1. To complete its life cycle, a biennial plant takes
- **a.** one growing season.
- **b.** two growing seasons.
- **c.** three growing seasons.
- **d.** more than three growing seasons.

_____ 2. The flowers of bread wheat, like all grass flowers, lack
- **a.** pistils and stamens.
- **b.** pistils and sepals.
- **c.** stamens and sepals.
- **d.** petals and sepals.

_____ 3. Which of the following is NOT a mineral nutrient that plants need?
- **a.** auxin
- **b.** sulfur
- **c.** nitrogen
- **d.** magnesium

_____ 4. The major difference between plant and animal development is that
- **a.** animals continue to develop even after they become adults.
- **b.** plants continue to develop throughout their lives.
- **c.** only plants have genes that guide their development.
- **d.** some animal cells can reverse their development.

_____ 5. The Dutch biologist Frits Went showed that the bending of plants toward light is caused by a chemical called
- **a.** auxin.
- **b.** agar.
- **c.** culm.
- **d.** ethylene.

_____ 6. A tropism is a growth response
- **a.** toward light.
- **b.** to touch.
- **c.** toward or away from a stimulus.
- **d.** toward gravity.

_____ 7. Many of a plant's responses to environmental stimuli are caused by
- **a.** the length of the nights.
- **b.** hormones.
- **c.** temperature.
- **d.** All of the above

Complete each statement by writing the correct term or phrase in the space provided.

8. Once water has entered the seed and the seed coat breaks, the seedling will

begin to grow if adequate _____ and _____

are available.

9. The plant tissues that result from primary growth are known as

_____ _____ .

Test Prep Pretest *continued*

10. Wheat grains are high in _____ , a sticky mixture of proteins that makes bread dough elastic.

11. Every year _____ _____ are usually formed by thick layers of secondary xylem.

12. Virtually all annuals are _____ plants, and they complete their life cycle within _____ growing season(s).

13. Apical meristems are located at the _____ of _____ and _____ .

14. A gaseous compound that _____ fruit ripening and loosens the fruit of cherries, blackberries, and blueberries is _____ .

15. A shoot that grows up out of the ground shows both positive _____ and negative _____ .

16. A condition in which a seed or a plant remains inactive even when conditions are suitable for growth is called _____ .

Read each question, and write your answer in the space provided.

17. What must happen before a seed can germinate?

_____

_____

_____

_____

18. How can new plants be grown in a tissue culture?

_____

_____

_____

_____

_____

_____

_____

Test Prep Pretest *continued*

19. List at least three mineral nutrients that are necessary for plant growth.

_____

_____

_____

20. Summarize how Frits Went demonstrated the presence of the chemical auxin in a shoot tip.

_____

_____

_____

_____

_____

_____

_____

Name _____ Class _____ Date _____

Vocabulary Review

Use the terms from the list below to fill in the blanks in the following passage.

acoelomates	ectoderm	hydrostatic skeleton
asymmetrical	endoderm	internal fertilization
bilateral symmetry	endoskeleton	mesoderm
blastula	exoskeleton	open circulatory system
body plan	external fertilization	phylogenetic tree
cephalization	gastrovascular cavity	pseudocoelomates
closed circulatory system	gills	radial symmetry
coelom	hermaphrodites	respiration
coelomates		

In all animals except sponges, the zygote undergoes cell divisions that form a(n)

(1) _____ , which eventually develops into three distinct layers

of cells, which are the **(2)** _____ , **(3)** _____ ,

and **(4)** _____ .

All animals have their own particular **(5)** _____

_____ , a term used to describe an animal's shape, symmetry,

and internal organization. Sponges are **(6)** _____ . The first

animals to evolve in the ancient oceans had **(7)** _____

_____ , having the body parts are arranged around a central axis.

The bodies of all other animals have distinct right and left halves. This is called

(8) _____ _____ . Most animals with this type of

symmetry also have evolved an anterior concentration of sensory structures and

nerves—a feature called **(9)** _____ .

Bilaterally symmetrical animals have different kinds of internal body plans

depending on whether they have a(n) **(10)** _____ , a body

cavity filled with fluid. Animals with no body cavity are called

(11) _____ . **(12)** _____ have a body cavity

located between the mesoderm and the endoderm. **(13)** _____

have a body cavity located entirely within the mesoderm, and the gut and other

internal organs are suspended within a fluid-filled coelom.

To visually represent the relationships among various groups of animals,

scientists often use a type of branching diagram called a(n)

(14) _____ _____ , which shows how animals are

related through evolution.

The digestive system enables animals to ingest and digest food. Simple ani-

mals have a(n) **(15)** _____ _____ , which has

only one opening. More complex animals have a digestive tract (gut) with a

mouth and an anus.

The uptake of oxygen and the release of carbon dioxide are called

(16) _____ and can take place only across a wet surface.

Examples are the damp skin of an earthworm, the **(17)** _____

of aquatic animals, or the lungs of land animals. In complex animals, a

system is needed to deliver oxygen and nutrients to the cells. In a(n)

(18) _____ _____ _____ , the

heart pumps a fluid into the body cavity and the fluid collects in open spaces in

the animal's body and is returned to the heart. In a(n) **(19)** _____

_____ _____ , the heart pumps blood through a

system of blood vessels. The blood remains in the blood vessels and materials

pass into and out of the blood vessels through diffusion.

An animal's skeleton provides a framework that supports its body and helps

protect its soft parts. Earthworms have a(n) **(20)** _____

_____ , which consists of water that is contained under pressure

in a coelom. Insects, clams, and crabs have a(n) **(21)** _____ ,

Vocabulary Review *continued*

which is a hard, external skeleton that encases the body of the animal. A(n)

(22) _____ is composed of a hard material, such as bone, and

is embedded within an animal.

In sexual reproduction, a new individual is formed by the union of a male and

a female gamete. Many simple invertebrates, including slugs and earthworms,

produce both types of gametes because they have both testes and ovaries. Such

animals are called **(23)** _____ . Most aquatic animals release the

male and female gametes near one another in the water, where fertilization

occurs. This method is called **(24)** _____ _____ .

In **(25)** _____ _____ , the union of the sperm

and egg occurs within the female's body.

Skills Worksheet

Test Prep Pretest

In the space provided, write the letter of the term or phrase that best completes each statement or best answers each question.

_____ 1. The cells of all animals are organized into structural and functional units called tissues EXCEPT for the cells of
    a. sponges.
    b. cnidarians.
    c. flatworms.
    d. roundworms.

_____ 2. All animals except sponges and single-celled organisms digest their food
    a. in the coelom.
    b. in a one-way gut.
    c. extracellularly.
    d. intracellularly.

_____ 3. An animal in which the space between the body wall and gut is completely filled with tissues and organs is called a(n)
    a. acoelomate.
    b. pseudocoelomate.
    c. coelomate.
    d. vertebrate.

_____ 4. An animal whose gut has only one opening has a(n)
    a. intervascular cavity.
    b. gastrovascular cavity.
    c. specialized digestive tract.
    d. one-way digestive system.

_____ 5. In an open circulatory system, the route of the blood is
    a. heart, blood vessels, tissues, heart.
    b. heart, open spaces, body cavity, tissues, heart.
    c. heart, blood vessels, heart.
    d. heart, blood vessels, body cavity, tissues, open spaces, heart.

_____ 6. Parthenogenesis is a method of
    a. sexual reproduction.
    b. fragmentation.
    c. asexual reproduction.
    d. fertilization.

_____ 7. Specialized areas for food storage and chemical digestion are found in a(n)
    a. excretory system.
    b. one-way digestive system.
    c. gastrovascular cavity.
    d. coelom.

_____ 8. What is the most accurate method of determining the evolutionary relationships of different animal species?
    a. by comparing their fossils
    b. by looking at a phylogenetic tree
    c. by comparing their size
    d. by comparing their DNA

Complete each statement by writing the correct term or phrase in the space provided.

9. Without a(n) _____ _____ , an animal could not eliminate the waste products of cellular metabolism.

10. The _____ _____ of an earthworm is formed from a fluid contained under pressure in a closed cavity.

11. A(n) _____ develops after a zygote undergoes cell division to form a hollow ball of cells.

12. In a bilaterally symmetrical animal, the top surface of the animal is referred to as _____ and the bottom surface as _____ . The front end of the animal is _____ and the back end is _____ .

13. Muscles, most of the skeleton, the circulatory system, reproductive organs, and excretory organs arise from the primary tissue layer called _____ .

14. A sea anemone's body plan is an example of _____ _____ because its body parts are arranged around a central axis.

15. An animal that is a(n) _____ has both ovaries and testes.

16. The ectoderm, endoderm, and mesoderm are called _____ _____ _____ because they give rise to all the tissues and organs of an adult body.

17. Most terrestrial animals do not respire with _____ because these tissues must be kept moist.

18. The _____ _____ contributed to the evolution of complex organs composed of more than one tissue type.

Test Prep Pretest *continued*

Read each question, and write your answer in the space provided.

19. Describe the organization of the animal kingdom and at least six physical characteristics scientists consider to determine the evolutionary relationships among animals.

_____

_____

_____

_____

_____

_____

_____

20. Explain why animals that use external fertilization must release large numbers of gametes.

_____

_____

_____

_____

_____

_____

_____

Vocabulary Review

In the space provided, write the letter of the description that best matches the term or phrase.

_____ 1. mesoglea

_____ 2. ostia

_____ 3. sessile

_____ 4. oscula

_____ 5. choanocytes

_____ 6. amoebocytes

_____ 7. spongin

_____ 8. spicules

_____ 9. gemmules

_____ 10. medusa

_____ 11. polyp

_____ 12. cnidocytes

_____ 13. nematocyst

_____ 14. basal disk

_____ 15. planula

_____ 16. proglottids

_____ 17. fluke

_____ 18. tegument

a. sponge cells that have irregular amoeba-like shapes

b. clusters of amoebocytes encased in protective coats

c. large openings in a sponge's body wall through which materials leave

d. resilient flexible protein fiber

e. free-floating life-form of a cnidarian

f. stinging cells located on tentacles of cnidarians

g. firmly attached to the sea bottom or other surface

h. body form of a cnidarian that is attached to a rock or some other object

i. a gel-like substance

j. small barbed harpoon inside a cnidocyte

k. flagellated cells also known as collar cells

l. larval stage of a hydrozoan

m. body sections of flatworms

n. parasitic flatworm

o. tiny needles of silica or calcium carbonate that form a sponge's skeleton

p. protective covering of endoparasitic flukes

q. area on *Hydra* that produces a sticky secretion

r. tiny openings or pores in a sponge's body wall through which materials enter

Test Prep Pretest

In the space provided, write the letter of the term or phrase that best completes each statement or best answers each question.

_____ 1. Support for most sponges is provided by a simple skeleton composed of protein fibers called
    a. spicules.   **c.** gemmules.
    b. spongin.   **d.** silica.

_____ 2. Which of the following is characteristic of the roundworm *Ascaris*?
    a. The eggs can live in soil for years.
    b. The eggs can block ducts leading from organs in the human body, such as the gallbladder.
    c. The eggs can travel to the lungs and cause respiratory distress.
    d. All of the above

_____ 3. The simplest animal that has a one-way digestive system is the
    a. fluke.   **c.** roundworm.
    b. flatworm.   **d.** trematode.

Questions 4–6 refer to the figure below, which shows *Dugesia*.

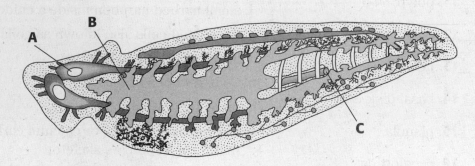

_____ 4. The structure labeled *A* is
    a. the brain.   **c.** the mouth.
    b. a nerve cord.   **d.** an eyespot.

_____ 5. The structure labeled *B* is
    a. the intestine.   **c.** the mouth.
    b. a flame cell.   **d.** an eyespot.

_____ 6. The structure labeled *C* is
    a. the intestine.   **c.** the mouth.
    b. a flame cell.   **d.** the anus.

In the space provided, write the letter of the description that best matches the term or phrase.

_____ **7.** amoebocyte

_____ **8.** gemmules

_____ **9.** planulae

_____ **10.** flame cells

_____ **11.** tegument

a. in planarians, specialized cells with beating tufts of cilia that draw water through pores to the outside of the worm's body

b. free-swimming cnidarian larvae

c. an amoeba-like cell in a sponge that moves through the body cells, supplying nutrients and removing wastes

d. thick protective covering of cells that protects endoparasites from being digested by their host

e. clusters of amoebocytes with protective coats that enable them to survive harsh conditions that may kill the adult sponge; produced by some freshwater sponges

Complete each statement by writing the correct term or phrase in the space provided.

12. Cnidarians have stinging cells called _____ for capturing prey.

13. The Portuguese man-of-war is a member of the class _____ .

14. Anthozoans typically have a stalklike body topped by a crown of

_____ .

15. *Schistosoma*, sometimes called a blood fluke, must live in a(n)

_____ before it can infect humans.

Read each question, and write your answer in the space provided.

16. Describe how sponge cells get nutrients.

_____

_____

_____

_____

_____

Test Prep Pretest *continued*

17. Describe the process of sexual reproduction in sponges.

_____

_____

_____

_____

_____

18. Describe the specialized features of the Portuguese man-of-war.

_____

_____

_____

_____

_____

_____

19. *Obelia* produces both polyps and gametes that join to produce planulae. Explain what the life of each form will be like.

_____

_____

_____

_____

_____

20. How can humans prevent hookworm infestation?

_____

_____

_____

_____

Name _____ Class _____ Date _____

Vocabulary Review

Use the terms and phrases from the list below to fill in the blanks in the following passage.

adductor muscles	nephridia	setae
cerebral ganglion	parapodia	siphons
foot	radula	trochophore
mantle	septa	visceral mass

Mollusks and annelids were probably the first major groups of organisms to develop a true coelom. Another feature shared by many mollusks and annelids is a larval stage called a(n) **(1)** _____, which develops from the fertilized egg.

The body cavity in mollusks is a true coelom and usually exhibits bilateral symmetry. Mollusks have many organ systems, which are contained in the **(2)** _____ _____ .

A(n) **(3)** _____ wraps around the visceral mass.

Every mollusk has a muscular region called a(n) **(4)** _____ .

Many mollusks have one or two shells, which protect their soft bodies. All mollusks, except bivalves, have a tonguelike organ called a(n)

(5) _____ .

Mollusks are the only coelomates without segmented bodies. Like round-worms, mollusks have a one-way digestive system. Mollusks use their coelom as a collecting place for waste-laden body fluids. Before leaving the body, this fluid passes into tiny tubular structures called **(6)** _____ .

Mollusks have a circulatory system, and most respire through gills.

| **Vocabulary Review** *continued*

Gastropods—snails and slugs—are primarily a marine group that has also very successfully invaded freshwater and terrestrial habitats. Most bivalves are marine, but some live in fresh water. All bivalves have a two-part hinged shell. Two thick **(7)** _____ _____ connect the valves, and when contracted, they cause the valves to close tightly.

Most bivalves are filter feeders, and many use their muscular foot to dig down into the sand. The cilia on the gills of a bivalve draw in sea water through hollow tubes called **(8)** _____ .

Annelids are easily recognized by their segments, which are visible externally as a series of ringlike structures along the length of their body. A well-developed primitive brain, called a(n) **(9)** _____ _____ , is located in one anterior segment. Internal body walls, called **(10)** _____ , separate the segments of most annelids.

Annelids have a body cavity that is a true coelom, and they have organ systems. Most annelids have external bristles called **(11)** _____ . Some annelids have fleshy appendages called **(12)** _____ . These two external characteristics are used to classify annelids.

Skills Worksheet)

Test Prep Pretest

In the space provided, write the letter of the term or phrase that best completes each statement or best answers each question.

_____ 1. The fertilized eggs of both mollusks and annelids develop into a distinct larval form called a
  a. polyp.
  b. veliger.
  c. trochophore.
  d. nudibranch.

_____ 2. Which of the following is NOT a characteristic of mollusks?
  a. acoelomate body structure
  b. bilateral symmetry
  c. organ systems
  d. three-part body plan

_____ 3. Annelids were the first organisms to exhibit
  a. a true coelom.
  b. organ systems.
  c. bilateral symmetry.
  d. segmentation.

_____ 4. All annelids have a(n)
  a. closed circulatory system and a radula.
  b. closed circulatory system and a mantle.
  c. closed circulatory system and a nerve cord.
  d. open circulatory system and a series of hearts.

_____ 5. Which of the following is NOT a characteristic of annelids?
  a. gills or lungs
  b. organ systems
  c. a highly specialized gut
  d. segmented bodies

_____ 6. When soil in the digestive tract of an earthworm leaves the crop, it passes to the
  a. pharynx.
  b. gizzard.
  c. esophagus.
  d. anus.

_____ 7. The movement of earthworms requires
  a. muscles lining the interior body wall.
  b. muscle contractions.
  c. traction provided by setae.
  d. All of the above

Complete each statement by writing the correct term or phrase in the space provided.

8. When the _____ muscles of a bivalve contract, they cause the valves to close forcefully.

9. Bivalves feed by sucking sea water through hollow tubes called

_____ .

10. The only living cephalopod species that has an outer shell is the

_____ .

Questions 11–13 refer to the figure below, which shows the structure of an earthworm.

11. The structure labeled *A*, called the _____ , grinds up soil

that the earthworm ingests.

12. The _____ _____ , labeled *B*,

coordinates the muscular activity of each body segment.

13. The earthworm anchors several of its segments by sinking its

_____ , labeled *C*, into the ground.

Read each question, and write your answer in the space provided.

14. What is a trochophore?

_____

_____

_____

_____

Name _____ Class _____ Date _____

15. Why are terrestrial snails more active when the air around them is moist?

_____

_____

_____

16. Describe the function of septa in annelids.

_____

_____

_____

17. How are cephalopods adapted as predators?

_____

_____

_____

18. In what basic way do the annelid and mollusk body plans differ?

_____

_____

_____

_____

19. How are annelids classified?

_____

_____

_____

_____

20. Why do earthworms require a moist environment?

_____

_____

_____

_____

Skills Worksheet

Vocabulary Review

Write the correct term from the list below in the space next to its definition.

appendages	Malpighian tubules	spinneret	thorax
cephalothorax	mandible	spiracle	tracheae
chelicerae	pedipalps		

_____ **1.** structures that extend from the body wall

_____ **2.** the midbody region

_____ **3.** head fused with thorax

_____ **4.** network of tubes through which many arthropods respire

_____ **5.** structure through which air enters a terrestrial arthropod's body

_____ **6.** excretory units of terrestrial arthropods

_____ **7.** mouthparts in the subphylum Chelicerata

_____ **8.** pairs of appendages modified to handle prey

_____ **9.** appendage that secretes strands of silk

_____ **10.** chewing mouthpart in the subphylum Uniramia

In the space provided, write the letter of the description that best matches the term or phrase.

_____**11.** molting

_____**12.** metamorphosis

_____**13.** chrysalis

_____**14.** pupa

_____**15.** nymph

_____**16.** caste

_____**17.** nauplius

_____**18.** compound eye

_____**19.** krill

a. the role played by an individual in a colony

b. the physical change of a young insect into an adult

c. a young insect that looks like a small, wingless adult

d. larval form of crustacean

e. stage in complete metamorphosis during which a young insect becomes an adult

f. a protective capsule

g. periodic shedding of exoskeleton

h. small marine crustacean

i. made of thousands of individual units

Name _____ Class _____ Date _____

Test Prep Pretest

In the space provided, write the letter of the term or phrase that best completes each statement or best answers each question.

_____ **1.** Subphylum Uniramia includes
  a. insects.
  b. millipedes.
  c. centipedes.
  d. All of the above

_____ **2.** All arachnids, except some mites, are
  a. insectivores.
  b. herbivores.
  c. carnivores.
  d. omnivores.

_____ **3.** Which of the following characteristics is NOT shared by all insects?
  a. three body sections
  b. five-part radial symmetry
  c. three pairs of legs
  d. one pair of antennae

_____ **4.** The head, thorax, and abdomen of mites
  a. are separate segmented sections.
  b. form two sections, the cephalothorax and the abdomen.
  c. are fused to form a single body.
  d. form two sections, the head and a fused thorax and abdomen.

_____ **5.** Spiders produce silk from
  a. spinnerets.
  b. mandibles.
  c. chelicerae.
  d. pedipalps.

In the space provided, write the letter of the description that best matches the term or phrase.

_____ **6.** exoskeleton

_____ **7.** spiracle

_____ **8.** Malpighian tubules

_____ **9.** swimmerets

a. the shell-like structure that encases the bodies of arthropods

b. appendages attached along the underside of the abdomen that are used by lobsters and crayfish for swimming and reproduction

c. fingerlike excretory organs

d. an opening that functions during respiration in many arthropods

Complete each statement by writing the correct term or phrase in the space provided.

10. An arthropod must shed its _____ to grow.

11. Infected deer ticks may spread _____ _____ .

12. The free-swimming nauplius is the _____ form of a crustacean.

Test Prep Pretest *continued*

Questions 13–15 refer to the figure below.

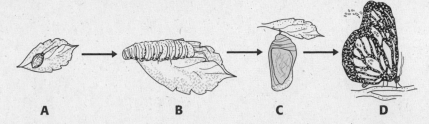

13. The process taking place in the figure above is _____

_____ .

14. The stage labeled *D* shows the _____ , while the stage

labeled *A* shows the _____ .

15. During this process, the _____ is enclosed within a

protective capsule called a(n) _____ , labeled *C*.

Read each question, and write your answer in the space provided.

16. Why do scientists think that arthropods and annelids share a common ancestor?

_____

_____

17. List three important characteristics of crustaceans.

_____

_____

18. Distinguish between centipedes and millipedes.

_____

_____

19. Describe the wings of grasshoppers.

_____

_____

20. List three ways in which the mouthparts of insects are adapted for different functions.

_____

_____

Skills Worksheet

Vocabulary Review

Write the correct term from the list below in the space next to its definition.

blastopore	ossicles	skin gills
deuterostome	protostome	water-vascular system

_____ 1. the opening to the outside during the gastrula stage of an embryo

_____ 2. an animal whose mouth develops from or near the blastopore

_____ 3. an animal whose anus develops from or near the blastopore

_____ 4. calcium-rich plates that make up the endoskeleton of an echinoderm

_____ 5. a water-filled system of interconnected canals and thousands of tiny, hollow tube feet

_____ 6. small, fingerlike projections that grow among the spines of an echinoderm where respiratory gases are exchanged

In the space provided, write the letter of the description that best matches the term or phrase.

_____ 7. chordate

_____ 8. notochord

_____ 9. pharyngeal slit

_____ 10. invertebrate chordate

a. opening that develops in the wall of the pharynx

b. chordate that does not have a backbone

c. animal that has a notochord

d. a stiff rod that develops along the back of an embryo

Test Prep Pretest

In the space provided, write the letter of the term or phrase that best completes each statement or best answers each question.

_____ 1. An animal whose mouth develops from the blastopore is called a
    a. deuterostome.
    c. cephalostome.
    b. protostome.
    d. pseudocoelom.

_____ 2. Echinoderms share all of the following characteristics EXCEPT
    a. an endoskeleton composed of ossicles.
    b. a radially symmetrical body plan in adulthood.
    c. a water-vascular system.
    d. a notochord.

_____ 3. The water-vascular system of echinoderms functions as a
    a. means of movement.
    b. gas exchange system.
    c. waste excretion system.
    d. All of the above

_____ 4. Chordates are characterized by all of the following EXCEPT
    a. radial symmetry.
    b. pharyngeal slits.
    c. a tail that extends beyond the anus.
    d. a dorsal, hollow nerve cord.

_____ 5. An invertebrate chordate is a member of the phylum Chordata and lacks which of the following?
    a. notochord
    b. tail
    c. backbone
    d. nerve cord

Complete each statement by writing the correct term or phrase in the space provided.

6. Many echinoderms crawl across the seafloor by means of a(n)

_____-_____ system.

7. Because echinoderms and chordates develop similarly as embryos, it is likely

that they are derived from a(n) _____

_____ .

8. In many echinoderms, respiration and waste removal are aided by

_____ _____ , which are small,

fingerlike projections that grow among the spines.

9. The echinoderm endoskeleton is composed of individual plates called

_____ .

10. The water-vascular system of an echinoderm is a series of interconnected

_____ and thousands of tiny, hollow _____

_____ .

11. Echinoderms have no head or brain, but they do have a central

_____ of _____ with branches that

extend into each of the arms.

12. Many species of sea stars have pincerlike structures called

_____ .

13. Unlike other echinoderms, _____ _____

have ossicles that are small and not fused together.

14. Of all the chordate characteristics, only _____

_____ are retained by adult tunicates.

15. Some tunicates reproduce asexually by _____ .

Name _____ Class _____ Date _____

Read each question, and write your answer in the space provided.

Questions 16 through 18 refer to the figure below.

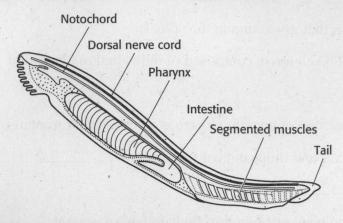

16. Identify the animal shown above.

_____

17. Based on the labeled structures, how would you know that this animal is a chordate?

_____

_____

_____

18. How would an adult tunicate differ from the animal shown above?

_____

_____

19. Describe how a sea star is able to move using its water-vascular system.

_____

_____

_____

_____

20. Describe the similarities between tunicates and lancelets.

_____

_____

_____

Skills Worksheet

Vocabulary Review

Complete the crossword puzzle using the clues provided.

ACROSS

1. describing animals that maintain a high, constant body temperature from heat produced by metabolism

3. extinct, spiny fish

5. describing animals that live on land

7. a single supercontinent that existed 200 million years ago

8. extinct crocodile-like dinosaur

DOWN

1. describing animals whose body temperature is determined by the temperature of the environment

2. lightweight, strong, and flexible tissue

3. jawless fish

4. individual segment of a backbone

6. extinct order of reptiles that probably gave rise to mammals

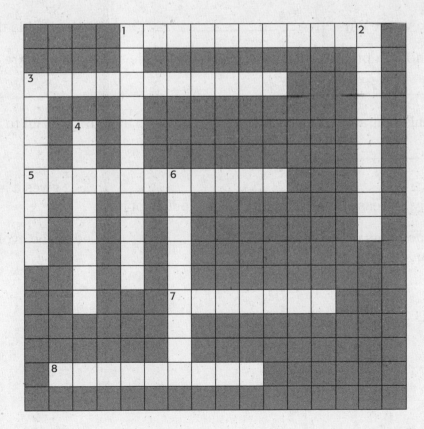

Vocabulary Review *continued*

In the space provided, write the letter of the description that best matches the term or phrase.

_____ **9.** primates

_____ **10.** prosimians

_____ **11.** diurnal

_____ **12.** opposable thumb

_____ **13.** hominids

a. can be bent inward toward fingers to hold an object

b. active during the day and sleep at night

c. group that includes prosimians, monkeys, apes, and humans

d. mostly night-active primates that live in trees

e. primates that walk upright on two legs

Complete each statement by writing the correct term or phrase in the space provided.

14. Monkeys are day-active _____ with opposable thumbs.

15. The modern primates that most closely resemble early primates are

_____ .

16. Animals that are active during the day and sleep at night are said to

be _____ .

17. A(n) _____ _____ gives a hand a greatly increased level of ability to manipulate objects.

18. The members of the group _____ led to the evolution of humans.

Name _____ Class _____ Date _____

Test Prep Pretest

In the space provided, write the letter of the term or phrase that best completes each statement or best answers each question.

_____ 1. The two distinct anatomical changes that set the earliest primates apart from their ancestors were
   a. opposable thumbs and color vision.
   b. large eyes and clawed, unbendable toes.
   c. grasping hands and binocular vision.
   d. color vision and grasping hands.

_____ 2. Which of the following is NOT a key adaptation that enabled fishes to dominate the oceans?
   a. paired fins   **c.** streamlined bodies
   b. lungs   **d.** strong jaws

_____ 3. In comparison to monkeys, apes have
   a. larger brains.
   b. smaller brains.
   c. longer tails.
   d. smaller brains and shorter tails.

_____ 4. Compared with modern humans, Neanderthals had
   a. a slightly larger brain, on average.
   b. a much smaller brain, on average.
   c. a taller body.
   d. less prominent brow ridges.

_____ 5. The pattern of bones in an amphibian's limbs resembles the pattern in a
   a. jawless fish.   **c.** lobe-finned fish.
   b. cartilaginous fish.   **d.** shark.

_____ 6. *Homo erectus*
   a. evolved in Africa and remained there.
   b. appeared 1 million years before Java man.
   c. gave rise to *Homo habilis.*
   d. walked upright and used tools.

_____ 7. Features that *Archaeopteryx* shared with dinosaurs include
   a. a breastbone.   **c.** teeth and solid bones.
   b. feathers.   **d.** a fused collarbone.

| **Test Prep Pretest** *continued*

Complete each statement by writing the correct term or phrase in the space provided.

8. All vertebrates have a(n) _____ circulatory system with

a(n) _____ heart.

9. Among the first primates to have opposable thumbs were

_____ .

10. *Homo* _____ became extinct after 500,000 years and had

a(n) _____ brain than the australopithecines.

11. By the end of the _____ period, almost all of the early
fishes had disappeared.

12. Animals that live on land are called _____ .

13. Mammals likely evolved from _____ , early reptiles that

were probably _____ .

14. The _____ of australopithecines had slightly greater
volume relative to body weight than those of apes.

15. The ability of some primates to walk _____ on

_____ _____ probably evolved in
response to environmental changes that occurred 15 million years ago.

Read each question, and write your answer in the space provided.

16. In what way are amphibians not fully adapted to life on land?

_____

_____

17. Why were dinosaurs able to become the dominant land vertebrates?

_____

_____

_____

_____

_____

_____

Test Prep Pretest *continued*

18. Describe the debate over whether dinosaurs were ectothermic or endothermic.

_____

_____

_____

_____

_____

19. What two characteristics distinguished australopithecines from apes?

_____

_____

20. Explain the two hypotheses of the origin of *Homo sapiens*.

_____

_____

_____

_____

_____

_____

_____

_____

Skills Worksheet

Vocabulary Review

Complete the crossword puzzle using the clues provided.

ACROSS

2. In a fish's gills, oxygen diffuses into the blood over the entire length of the capillaries due to _____ flow.

4. covers the gills on each side of the head

7. The _____ line extends along each side of a bony fish's body and allows the fish to perceive its position and rate of movement.

8. an internal, baglike respiratory organ

11. A swim _____ enables bony fishes to regulate their buoyancy.

DOWN

1. Oxygen-rich blood is carried from an amphibian's lungs to its heart by the _____ veins.

3. tubelike unit in a kidney

5. a fish with a completely symmetrical tail, highly mobile fins, and very thin scales

6. Each gill is made up of rows of fingerlike projections called gill _____ .

9. A _____ slit is an opening at the rear of the cheek cavity.

10. separates the amphibian atrium into right and left halves

Name _____ Class _____ Date _____

Test Prep Pretest

In the space provided, write the letter of the term or phrase that best completes each statement or best answers each question.

_____ 1. The major respiratory organ of a fish is the
    a. swim bladder.   **c.** gill.
    b. lung.   **d.** nephron.

_____ 2. Depending on the species, fish can reproduce through
    a. internal fertilization.   **c.** conjugation.
    b. spawning.   **d.** Both (a) and (b)

_____ 3. Lampreys and hagfishes are the only remaining
    a. jawless fishes.   **c.** lobe-finned fishes.
    b. cartilaginous fishes.   **d.** bony fishes

_____ 4. Members of the order Apoda do NOT
    a. use cutaneous respiration.   **c.** have legs.
    b. lay eggs.   **d.** bear live young.

_____ 5. Compared with that of a fish, a frog's cerebrum is
    a. less complex.   **c.** smaller.
    b. more complex.   **d.** Both (b) and (c)

Questions 6 and 7 refer to the figure at right, which shows the structure of a bony fish.

_____ 6. The structure labeled *A*
    is the
    a. dorsal fin.
    b. gill filament.
    c. operculum.
    d. lateral line.

_____ 7. The structure labeled *B*
    is called the
    a. pectoral fin.   **c.** pelvic fin.
    b. operculum.   **d.** jaw.

Complete each statement by writing the correct term or phrase in the space provided.

8. Fishes respire by using _____ .

9. A shark's teeth are actually modified _____ .

Name _____ Class _____ Date _____

10. In an amphibian, the _____ _____ carry oxygen-rich blood from the lungs to the heart.

11. All fishes have a(n) _____ _____ that surrounds the spinal cord.

12. In amphibians, one circulatory loop carries blood from the heart to the

_____ , while a second loop carries blood to the rest of the body.

13. The large size of the _____ _____ in the yellow perch's brain indicates the importance of vision to this fish.

14. Tubelike units called _____ in the kidneys of a fish regulate salt and water balance.

15. Salamanders are members of the order _____ .

16. The pattern of movement of water and blood through a fish's gills is called

_____ _____ .

Read each question, and write your answer in the space provided.

17. What is countercurrent flow, and why is it important to a fish?

_____

_____

_____

_____

_____

18. Describe the role of the tympanic membrane in a leopard frog's sense of balance.

_____

_____

_____

_____

_____

┃ Test Prep Pretest *continued*

19. How do lampreys and hagfishes feed?

_____

_____

_____

20. What information does a bony fish get from its lateral line system?

_____

_____

_____

Vocabulary Review

In the space provided, write the letter of the description that best matches the term or phrase.

_____ **1.** amniotic egg

_____ **2.** oviparous

_____ **3.** ovoviviparous

_____ **4.** carapace

_____ **5.** plastron

a. top part of the shell of a turtle

b. encloses the embryo in a watery environment

c. bottom part of the shell of a turtle

d. meaning the female retains eggs within her body until shortly before or after hatching

e. meaning the young hatch from eggs

Complete each statement by writing the correct term or phrase in the space provided.

6. The body of a young bird is covered by _____ feathers.

7. The body of an adult bird gets its shape from _____ feathers.

8. A bird protects and waterproofs its feathers by pulling them through its beak and covering them with oil from its _____

_____ .

Skills Worksheet)

Test Prep Pretest

In the space provided, write the letter of the term or phrase that best completes each statement or best answers each question.

_____ **1.** Tuataras are members of the reptile order
  a. Chelonia.
  b. Squamata.
  c. Rhynchocephalia.
  d. Crocodilia.

_____ **2.** In the raising of their young, crocodiles most closely resemble
  a. turtles.
  b. lizards.
  c. snakes.
  d. birds.

_____ **3.** All reptiles EXCEPT crocodilians have
  a. a partially divided ventricle.
  b. lungs.
  c. overlapping scales.
  d. watertight skin.

_____ **4.** Which of the following is NOT true of a turtle's shell?
  a. Vertebrae are fused to the inside of the carapace.
  b. The shell provides support for muscle attachment.
  c. The carapace is always dome shaped.
  d. The shell is made of fused plates of bone.

_____ **5.** The second chamber in the stomach of a bald eagle is known as the
  a. crop.
  b. gizzard.
  c. esophagus.
  d. cloaca.

In the space provided, write the letter of the description that best matches the term or phrase.

_____ **6.** contour feathers

_____ **7.** plastron

_____ **8.** Jacobson's organs

_____ **9.** carapace

a. detect odor of chemicals to help snakes follow prey

b. give an adult bird its shape

c. the bottom part of a turtle or tortoise shell

d. the top part of a turtle or tortoise shell

Test Prep Pretest *continued*

Complete each statement by writing the correct term or phrase in the space provided.

10. Because the _____ in a bird's heart is completely divided, oxygen-rich and oxygen-poor blood are kept completely _____ .

11. A timber rattlesnake's venom contains _____ , which destroy red blood cells and cause internal hemorrhaging.

12. A long, flattened, rounded bill, as found in _____, is adapted for sieving.

13. Feathers are modified reptilian _____ .

14. Most reptiles cannot live in avery cold regions because they are

    _____ .

15. Reptiles, birds, and three species of mammals reproduce by means of

    _____ eggs, which is evidence that they share a

    common _____ .

16. Many reptiles are _____ , meaning their young hatch from eggs.

17. Some species of snakes and lizards are _____ , which means the female retains the eggs within her body until shortly before hatching, or the eggs may hatch within the female's body.

Read each question, and write your answer in the space provided.

18. List the four orders of present-day reptiles, and give an example of each.

    _____

    _____

    _____

    _____

    _____

| Test Prep Pretest *continued*

19. Describe the structure and function of a turtle's shell.

_____

_____

_____

_____

_____

_____

20. Which is more efficient—a bird lung or a reptile lung? Explain.

_____

_____

_____

_____

_____

_____

Skills Worksheet

Vocabulary Review

Complete each statement by writing the correct term or phrase in the space provided.

1. A(n) _____ is a filament composed mainly of dead cells filled with the protein keratin.

2. Mammary _____ produce a nutrient-rich energy source for nourishing young after their birth.

3. The time when a mother stops nursing her young is called

_____ .

4. An organ called the _____ allows the diffusion of nutrients and oxygen from the mother's blood into the blood of a developing fetus.

5. The period of time between fertilization and birth is called the

_____ _____ .

6. Mammals with hoofs are classified as _____ .

7. Some mammals regurgitate partly digested food, called

_____ , rechew it, and swallow it again for further digestion.

Name _____ Class _____ Date _____

Test Prep Pretest

In the space provided, write the letter of the term or phrase that best completes each statement or best answers each question.

_____ 1. Which of the following is NOT a characteristic of mammals?
a. hair
b. specialized teeth
c. ectothermic metabolism
d. mammary glands

_____ 2. Grizzly bears are able to eat vegetation because they have
a. a high metabolic rate.
b. a layer of fat.
c. a multichambered stomach.
d. rounded molar teeth with a wrinkled surface.

_____ 3. All female mammals have
a. a marsupium.
b. mammary glands.
c. pouches.
d. nipples.

_____ 4. Incisors are used for
a. biting and cutting.
b. stabbing and holding.
c. crushing and grinding.
d. Both (a) and (b)

Complete each statement by writing the correct term or phrase in the space provided.

5. Female monotremes produce _____ with leathery shells and incubates them with body heat.

6. A(n) _____ is a filament composed mainly of dead cells filled with the protein keratin.

7. The four types of mammalian teeth are _____ , _____ , _____ , and _____ .

8. The only animals that have hair are _____ .

9. The chest or abdomen of female mammals has _____ glands that produce milk for their young.

10. Grizzly bears rely primarily on their sense of _____ to find food.

11. Respiration in mammals is aided by the _____ , a sheet of muscle at the bottom of the rib cage.

12. The length of time between fertilization and birth is the

_____   _____ .

13. The duckbill platypus and two species of echidnas are the only living

_____ .

14. The majority of mammalian species in Australia and New Guinea are

_____ .

15. Placental mammals remain in the _____ through a relatively long gestation period, during which they receive nourishment through the _____ .

In the space provided, write the letter of the description that best matches the term or phrase.

_____ **16.** Order Insectivora

_____ **17.** Order Chiroptera

_____ **18.** Order Proboscidea

_____ **19.** Order Hyracoidea

_____ **20.** Order Endentata

_____ **21.** Order Perissodactyla

_____ **22.** Order Carnivora

a. have elongated nose; largest land animals alive today

b. toothless or have poorly developed teeth without enamel; includes armadillos

c. odd number of toes within their hooves; no rumen

d. only mammals capable of true flight

e. most similar to ancestors of placental mammals; extremely high metabolic rate

f. rabbitlike body; four hooved toes on the front feet and three on the back feet

g. extremely intelligent; excellent sense of smell, vision, and hearing

Test Prep Pretest *continued*

Read each question, and write your answer in the space provided.

23. Compare the degree of development and feeding habits of newborn monotremes, marsupials, and placental mammals.

_____

_____

_____

_____

_____

_____

_____

_____

_____

24. Why are there many marsupials in the Australian region and only one in North America?

_____

_____

_____

_____

_____

_____

_____

25. List at least three functions of hair.

_____

_____

_____

Skills Worksheet

Vocabulary Review

Complete each statement by writing the correct term or phrase in the space provided.

1. A(n) _____ is an action or series of actions performed by an animal in response to a stimulus.

2. Genetically programmed behavior (behavior influenced by genes) is often

called _____ _____ .

3. Innate behavior is called _____

_____ _____

_____ when the action always occurs in the same way.

4. The development of behaviors through experience is called

_____ .

5. Learning by association is called _____ .

6. The ability to analyze a problem and think of a possible solution is called

_____ .

7. Learning that can occur only during a specific period early in the life of an

animal and cannot be changed once learned is called

_____ .

8. An evolutionary mechanism in which traits that increase the ability of

individuals to attract or acquire mates appear with increased frequency

is called _____ _____ .

Skills Worksheet

Test Prep Pretest

In the space provided, write the letter of the term or phrase that best completes each statement or best answers each question.

_____ 1. Animal signals are used to
   a. influence an animal's behavior.
   b. solicit play.
   c. attract a mate.
   d. All of the above

_____ 2. Scientists who question the reasons a behavior exists are asking
   a. a "how" question.
   b. a "why" question.
   c. about the evolution of behavior.
   d. Both (b) and (c)

_____ 3. Sexual selection is a(n)
   a. innate behavior.
   b. evolutionary mechanism.
   c. behavioral signal.
   d. genetic trait.

_____ 4. In some animals, extreme traits for acquiring a mate include
   a. horns, antlers, and manes.
   b. the ability to learn.
   c. complex brain structure.
   d. All of the above

_____ 5. Which of the following is NOT a signal?
   a. feeding   **c.** color
   b. sound   **d.** scent

Question 6 refers to the figure at right.

_____ 6. The bird providing
   food to its young is
   engaging in
   a. foraging behavior.
   b. parental care.
   c. imprinting.
   d. territorial behavior.

_____ **7.** Vocal communication is most developed in
    a. birds.
    b. carnivores.
    c. marine animals.
    d. primates.

In the space provided, write the letter of the description that best matches the term or phrase.

_____ **8.** imprinting

_____ **9.** foraging behavior

_____ **10.** innate behavior

_____ **11.** conditioning

_____ **12.** territorial behavior

_____ **13.** signal

_____ **14.** operant conditioning

_____ **15.** habituation

a. locating, obtaining, and consuming food

b. protecting a resource for exclusive use

c. occurs only during a specific period early in an animal's life

d. used to influence another animal's behavior

e. a frequent, harmless stimulus is ignored

f. genetically programmed behavior

g. trial-and-error learning under highly controlled conditions

h. learning by association

Complete each statement by writing the correct term or phrase in the space provided.

16. A(n) _____ is an action or series of actions performed by an animal in response to a stimulus.

17. To understand the factors that trigger or control a behavior, a scientist asks a(n) _____ question.

18. When new male lions in a pride kill cubs of other males, they are demonstrating a behavior influenced by _____ _____ , which favors traits that benefit the _____ and not the species.

19. When rats locked in a box learned to depress a lever to get food, they demonstrated _____ _____ in a famous study conducted by B. F. Skinner.

Test Prep Pretest *continued*

20. Birds flying south for the winter are demonstrating _____

_____ .

21. When Pavlov's dogs learned to _____ a ringing bell with

meat powder, which caused them to salivate, they demonstrated

_____ _____ .

Read each question, and write your answer in the space provided.

22. Explain how imprinting in ducks and geese is influenced by both heredity
and learning.

_____

_____

_____

_____

23. What is the difference between a "how" and a "why" behavioral question?
Give an example of each.

_____

_____

_____

_____

24. List five types of signals and five methods animals can use to send and
receive signals.

_____

_____

_____

_____

25. Explain the difference between habituation and classical conditioning.

_____

_____

_____

_____

Name _____ Class _____ Date _____

Vocabulary Review

In the space provided, write the letter of the description that best matches the term or phrase.

_____ 1. epithelial tissue

_____ 2. nervous tissue

_____ 3. muscle tissue

_____ 4. connective tissue

_____ 5. body cavities

a. carries information throughout the body

b. provides support, protection, and insulation

c. fluid-filled spaces that contain major body organs

d. enables the movement of body structures

e. lines most body surfaces

Complete each statement by writing the correct term or phrase in the space provided.

6. The _____ _____ includes bones of the skull, spine, ribs, and sternum.

7. The _____ _____ includes bones of the arms, legs, pelvis, and shoulder.

8. Bone _____ is soft tissue inside bones that begins the manufacture of blood cells.

9. Bones are surrounded by a tough exterior membrane called the

   _____ that contains blood vessels that supply nutrients

   to bones.

10. Hollow channels that contain blood vessels that enter bone through the

    periosteum are called _____ _____ .

11. Bone cells called _____ maintain the mineral content of bone.

12. A disease that results in brittle bones and that affects more women than men

    is _____ , meaning "brittle bone."

13. A junction between two or more bones is called a(n) _____ .

14. Bones of a joint are held together by strong bands of connective tissue

    called _____ .

| Vocabulary Review *continued*

Use the terms from the list below to fill in the blanks in the following passage.

actin   myofibrils   sarcomere

extensor   myosin   tendons

flexor

Most skeletal muscles are attached to bones by strips of dense connective

tissue called **(15)** _____ . One muscle in a pair of muscles

pulls a bone in one direction, and the other muscle pulls the bone in the opposite

direction. A(n) **(16)** _____ muscle causes a joint to bend,

and a(n) **(17)** _____ muscle causes a joint to straighten.

Muscle tissue contains large amounts of protein filaments called

(18) _____ and **(19)** _____ , which

enable muscles to contract. Each muscle fiber is made of small cylindrical struc-

tures called **(20)** _____ , which have alternating light and

dark bands when viewed under a microscope. In the center of each light band is a

Z line, which anchors actin filaments. The area between the two Z lines is called

a(n) **(21)** _____ , the functional unit of muscle contraction.

In the space provided, write the letter of the description that best matches the term or phrase.

_____ **22.** epidermis

_____ **23.** keratin

_____ **24.** melanin

_____ **25.** dermis

_____ **26.** subcutaneous tissue

_____ **27.** hair follicle

_____ **28.** sebum

a. protein that makes skin tough and waterproof

b. functional layer of skin that lies just beneath the epidermis

c. the outermost layer of skin

d. oily secretion that lubricates the skin

e. made mostly of fat

f. pigment that helps determine skin color

g. produces individual hairs

Skills Worksheet

Test Prep Pretest

In the space provided, write the letter of the term or phrase that best completes each statement or best answers each question.

_____ 1. From simplest to most complex, the four levels of structural organization of the human body are as follows:
  a. tissues, cells, organs, organ systems
  b. cells, tissues, organs, organ systems
  c. organ systems, tissues, cells, organs
  d. cells, organs, tissues, organ systems

_____ 2. Types of connective tissue include all of the following EXCEPT
  a. blood.   **c.** fat.
  b. bone.   **d.** muscle.

_____ 3. Which of the following would likely occur if endothermy were disrupted?
  a. Body temperature could not be maintained.
  b. Strenuous physical activity would be difficult.
  c. Enzymes would be inactivated.
  d. All of the above

_____ 4. The appendicular skeleton includes bones of the
  a. cranium.   **c.** pelvis.
  b. spine.   **d.** ribs.

_____ 5. In early development, bone tissue is made mostly of
  a. groups of osteocytes.   **c.** periosteum.
  b. bone marrow.   **d.** cartilage.

In the space provided, write the letter of the description that best matches the term or phrase.

_____ 6. compact bone

_____ 7. spongy bone

_____ 8. red bone marrow

_____ 9. yellow bone marrow

_____ 10. periosteum

_____ 11. cartilage

_____ 12. Haversian canals

_____ 13. osteocytes

a. maintain mineral content of bone

b. template tissue for bone formation

c. site of blood cell production

d. channels containing blood vessels in concentric rings of compact bone

e. dense bone that provides a great deal of support

f. tough membrane surrounding bones

g. site of fat storage

h. loosely structured bone

Test Prep Pretest *continued*

Complete each statement by writing the correct term or phrase in the space provided.

14. The excretory system includes the kidneys, _____

_____ , ureters, and the _____ .

15. Osteoporosis can be delayed or prevented by _____

and a diet containing ample _____ .

16. A muscle fiber contains many bundles of cylindrical structures called

_____ .

17. When oxygen is plentiful, the ATP used to power muscle contractions is

supplied by _____ processes. As oxygen becomes

depleted, ATP is supplied by _____ processes.

18. A pigment found in the epidermis, _____ , absorbs UV
radiation and helps determine skin color.

19. Hair consists mostly of dead cells filled with the protein called

_____ , the same protein that makes the skin
tough and waterproof.

20. The dermis contains _____ _____ ,
which help regulate body temperature, either by radiating heat into the air
or by helping to insulate the body.

21. The most common type of skin cancer originates in cells of the

_____ that do not produce pigments.

22. Acne is caused by excessive secretion of _____ , an oily
secretion that lubricates the skin, by oil glands.

Test Prep Pretest *continued*

Read each question, and write your answer in the space provided.

23. Describe the three main types of joints, and give an example of each.

_____

_____

_____

_____

_____

_____

_____

24. Describe the interaction of myosin and actin during a muscle contraction.

_____

_____

_____

_____

_____

25. Differentiate between the epidermis, the dermis, and subcutaneous tissue.

_____

_____

_____

_____

_____

_____

Name _____ Class _____ Date _____

Vocabulary Review

Use the terms from the list below to fill in the blanks in the following passage.

ABO blood group system   lymphatic system   Rh factor

anemia   plasma   valves

arteries   platelets   veins

capillaries   red blood cells   white blood cells

cardiovascular system

The **(1)** _____ _____ transports

materials throughout the body and distributes heat. Blood circulation describes

the route blood takes as it leaves and then returns to the heart. **(2)** Blood vessels

that carry blood away from the heart are called _____ . From

the arteries, the blood passes into a network of smaller arteries called arterioles.

Eventually, the blood is pushed through to the **(3)** _____ ,

which are tiny blood vessels that allow the exchange of gases, nutrients, hor-

mones, and other molecules traveling in the blood. After leaving the capillaries,

the blood flows into small vessels called venules before emptying into larger

vessels called **(4)** _____ , which are blood vessels that carry

the blood back to the heart. Most veins have one-way **(5)** _____ ,

which are flaps of tissue that prevent the backflow of blood.

The **(6)** _____ _____ is a system

of the body that collects and recycles fluids that leak from the cardiovascular

system. It is also involved in fighting infections.

About 60 percent of the total volume of blood is **(7)** _____ .

Most of the cells that make up blood are **(8)** _____

_____ _____ . An abnormality in the

number or function of these cells results in **(9)** _____ , which

means that the oxygen-carrying ability of the blood is reduced.

Vocabulary Review *continued*

(10) The cells whose primary job is to defend the body against disease are

_____ _____ _____ .

(11) Cell fragments called _____ play an important role in

the clotting of blood.

Occasionally, an injury or a disorder is so serious that a person must receive

blood or blood components from another person. The blood of the recipient and

that of the donor must be compatible. Under the **(12)** _____

_____ _____ _____ ,

the primary blood types are A, B, AB, and O. The letters *A* and *B* refer to complex

carbohydrates on the surface of red blood cells that act as antigens. Another

important antigen is called the **(13)** _____ _____ .

In the space provided, write the letter of the description that best matches the term or phrase.

_____ **14.** atrium

_____ **15.** ventricle

_____ **16.** vena cava

_____ **17.** aorta

_____ **18.** coronary arteries

_____ **19.** sinoatrial node

_____ **20.** blood pressure

_____ **21.** pulse

_____ **22.** heart attack

_____ **23.** stroke

_____ **24.** pharynx

_____ **25.** larynx

_____ **26.** trachea

_____ **27.** bronchi

_____ **28.** alveoli

_____ **29.** diaphragm

a. the first arteries to branch from the aorta

b. chamber that pumps blood away from the heart

c. a small cluster of cardiac muscle cells; initiate heart contraction

d. the force exerted by blood as it moves through the blood vessels

e. sends blood to the coronary arteries and the rest of the body

f. a series of pressure waves within an artery

g. chamber that receives blood returning to the heart

h. when an area of the heart muscle stops working

i. vessel that collects oxygen-poor blood from the body

j. when an area of the brain does not receive enough blood

k. a long, straight tube in the chest cavity through which air passes

l. two small tubes that lead to the lungs

m. the voice box

n. a muscle at the bottom of the rib cage

o. a muscular tube in the upper throat

p. air sacs where gases are exchanged

Skills Worksheet

Test Prep Pretest

In the space provided, write the letter of the term or phrase that best completes each statement or best answers each question.

_____ 1. The actual exchange of materials between the blood and the cells of the body occurs in the

   a. arteries.   **c.** veins.

   b. arterioles.   **d.** capillaries.

_____ 2. When fluids leak out of the cardiovascular system, they are returned by the

   a. respiratory system.   **c.** endocrine system.

   b. lymphatic system.   **d.** digestive system.

_____ 3. Blood type is determined by the presence or absence of

   a. A and B antigens dissolved in the blood plasma.

   b. A and O antigens on the surface of red blood cells.

   c. A and B antigens on the surface of red blood cells.

   d. A and B antigens on the surface of white blood cells.

_____ 4. The blood pumped from the heart to the lungs is transported through

   a. the pulmonary circulation loop.

   b. the systemic circulation loop.

   c. both the pulmonary and systemic loops.

   d. neither the pulmonary nor the systemic loop.

_____ 5. As the left ventricle contracts, the blood is prevented from moving back into the left atrium by

   a. a one-way valve.

   b. the superior vena cava.

   c. the inferior vena cava.

   d. the pulmonary veins.

Complete each statement by writing the correct term or phrase in the space provided.

6. Carbon dioxide is an example of a(n) _____

   _____ transported by the cardiovascular system to

   excretory organs and tissues.

7. White blood cells, or _____, are the primary cells of the immune system.

Test Prep Pretest *continued*

8. The heart receives blood in the two _____ and pumps

blood away using the two _____ .

9. The _____ _____ in the right atrium

initiates each heart contraction.

10. The pressure that is measured during relaxation of the heart is called

_____ pressure, and the pressure that is measured upon

contraction of the ventricles is called _____ pressure.

11. When blood pressure becomes too high, a condition called

_____ results.

12. The _____ are suspended in the chest cavity and are

bound on the sides by the ribs and on the bottom by the diaphragm.

13. The alveoli are connected to the bronchi by a network of tiny tubes called

_____ .

14. During breathing, _____ occurs when the diaphragm and

rib cage return to their relaxed position.

15. The involuntary regulation of breathing is due to special

_____ in the brain and circulatory system.

16. A disease of the respiratory system that has been linked to cigarette smoking

is _____ .

Read each question, and write your answer in the space provided.

17. List the main plasma ions, and describe their functions.

_____

_____

_____

_____

_____

18. How does lymph move through the lymphatic system?

_____

_____

_____

_____

_____

19. How are oxygen and carbon dioxide transported in the blood?

_____

_____

_____

_____

_____

20. What is one factor that stimulates receptors in the brain, causing an increase in the breathing rate?

_____

_____

Skills Worksheet

Vocabulary Review

Complete each statement by writing the correct term or phrase in the space provided.

1. A(n) _____ is a substance the body needs for energy, growth, repair, and maintenance.

2. The process of breaking down food into molecules the body can use is called _____ .

3. A(n) _____ is the amount of heat energy required to raise the temperature of 1 g of water 1°C (1.8°F).

4. Organic substances that are necessary, in trace amounts, for the normal metabolic functioning of the body are called _____ .

5. Inorganic substances that are necessary to make certain body structures and substances, to continue normal nerve and muscle function, and to maintain osmotic balance are called _____ .

In the space provided, write the letter of the description that best matches the term or phrase.

_____ **6.** amylase

_____ **7.** esophagus

_____ **8.** pepsin

_____ **9.** lipase

_____ **10.** villi

_____ **11.** colon

a. the large intestine

b. fine, fingerlike projections in the small intestine

c. pancreatic enzyme that digests fat

d. a long tube that connects the mouth to the stomach

e. a digestive enzyme secreted by the stomach

f. an enzyme in saliva that breaks down carbohydrates

❚ Vocabulary Review *continued*

Use the terms from the list below to fill in the blanks in the following passage.

excretion   ureters   urinary bladder
nephrons   urethra   urine
urea

The process that rids the body of toxic chemicals, excess water, salts, and

carbon dioxide and that maintains osmotic and pH balances is called

(12) _____ . The organs of excretion are the lungs, the kid-

neys, and the skin. The liver plays a role in excretion because it converts ammo-

nia, a toxic nitrogen-containing waste, to **(13)** _____ , which

is a much less toxic waste.

   The tiny tubes in the kidneys with cup-shaped capsules surrounding

a tight ball of capillaries that filter wastes from the blood are

(14) _____ . These tubes retain useful molecules, and they

produce **(15)** _____ . Urine is carried from the kidneys into

the **(16)** _____ _____ by tubes called

(17) _____ .Urine leaves the body through a tube called the

(18) _____ .

Name _____ Class _____ Date _____

Test Prep Pretest

In the space provided, write the letter of the term or phrase that best completes each statement or best answers each question.

_____ **1.** A substance needed by the body for energy, growth, repair, and maintenance is called a(n)
   a. fatty acid.   **c.** nutrient.
   b. amino acid.   **d.** calorie.

_____ **2.** All of the following are nutrients found in food EXCEPT
   a. plasma.   **c.** proteins.
   b. carbohydrates.   **d.** vitamins.

_____ **3.** A diet high in saturated fats can be linked to which of the following?
   a. kidney failure
   b. anorexia nervosa
   c. bulimia
   d. high blood cholesterol levels

_____ **4.** According to the USDA food guide pyramid, a person should obtain
the most servings per day from
   a. fruits.
   b. breads, cereals, rice, and pasta.
   c. fats, oils, and sweets.
   d. milk, yogurt, and cheese.

_____ **5.** Amylases begin the breakdown of carbohydrates into
   a. fatty acids.   **c.** amino acids.
   b. polypeptides.   **d.** simple sugars.

_____ **6.** In the stomach, single protein strands are cut into smaller amino acid
chains by the digestive enzyme called
   a. amylase.   **c.** lipase.
   b. pepsin.   **d.** gastrin.

_____ **7.** The products of digestion are absorbed into the bloodstream
through the
   a. villi and microvilli of the small intestine.
   b. rectum of the large intestine.
   c. gallbladder.
   d. sphincter of the stomach.

_____ **8.** Bile, which emulsifies fat globules, is produced by the
   a. pancreas.   **c.** liver.
   b. gallbladder.   **d.** duodenum.

_____ 9. During the metabolism of proteins and nucleic acids, the toxic waste product that is formed is
   a. urea.
   b. urine.
   c. carbon dioxide.
   d. ammonia.

_____10. The end result of the filtration, reabsorption, and secretion processes in the nephrons is
   a. water.
   b. carbon dioxide.
   c. urine.
   d. urea.

_____11. Urine leaves the bladder and exits the body through a tube called the
   a. urethra.
   b. ureter.
   c. kidney.
   d. nephron.

Questions 12–14 refer to the figure at right.

_____12. The blood-filtering unit in the figure is called a(n)
   a. villus.
   b. nephron.
   c. urethra.
   d. microvillus.

_____13. The structure labeled *A* is called the
   a. loop.
   b. glomerulus.
   c. renal tubule.
   d. Bowman's capsule.

_____14. The structure labeled *C* is called the
   a. loop of Henle.
   b. glomerulus.
   c. renal tubule.
   d. Bowman's capsule.

Complete each statement by writing the correct term or phrase in the space provided.

15. Excess carbohydrates are stored as _____ in the liver and in some muscle tissue.

16. Successive rhythmic waves of contraction of the smooth muscles around the

   esophagus, called _____ _____ ,
   move the food toward the stomach.

17. Of the four functions of the digestive system, the process of getting rid of

undigested molecules and waste occurs in the _____

_____ .

18. The wall of the large intestine absorbs mostly _____

_____ and _____ .

19. When you exhale, _____ _____

and some water are excreted by the lungs.

20. A procedure for filtering the blood called _____

_____ can prolong the lives of many people with

damaged kidneys.

Read each question, and write your answer in the space provided.

21. Describe the connection between heart disease and the USDA food pyramid's
daily serving recommendation for fats.

_____

_____

22. How do the liver and the pancreas differ from other digestive organs?

_____

_____

23. Describe the similarities and differences between a mineral and a vitamin.

_____

_____

24. Name two organs other than the kidney that are involved in excretion, and
describe what each organ excretes.

_____

_____

25. Relate the role of water in maintaining a healthy body.

_____

_____

_____

Name _____ Class _____ Date _____

Vocabulary Review

In the blanks provided, fill in the letters of the term or phrase being described.

1. a disease-causing agent
   _ A _ _ _ _ _ _

2. layers of epithelial tissue that serve as barriers to pathogens and produce chemical defense
   M _ _ _ _ _   M _ _ _ _ _ _ _ _

3. a series of events that suppress infection
   _ _ _ L _ _ _ _ _ _ _   _ E _ _ _ _ _ _

4. chemical that causes local blood vessels to dilate
   _ _ _ T _ _ _ _ _

5. a defense mechanism with 20 different proteins
   _ _ _ _ _ _ M _ _ _   Y _ _ _ _ _

6. a protein released by cells infected with viruses
   _ _ _ _ _ F _ _ _ _

7. a white blood cell that releases chemicals that kill pathogens
   N _ _ _ _ _ _ _ _ _

8. a white blood cell that ingests and kills pathogens
   _ _ _ R _ _ _ _ _ _

9. destroys an infected cell by puncturing its membrane
   N _ _ _ _ _ _ _   _ _ _ L _ _   _ _ _ L

Use the terms and phrases from the list below to fill in the blanks in the following passage.

   antibodies   B cells   helper T cells
   antigens   cytotoxic T cells   plasma cells

White blood cells are produced in bone marrow and circulate in blood and

lymph. Four main kinds of white blood cells are involved in the immune

response. Macrophages consume pathogens and infected cells. The cells that

attack and kill infected cells are called (10) _____

_____ . These cells, (11) _____ , label

invaders for later destruction by macrophages. White blood cells that activate both cytotoxic T cells and B cells are **(12)** _____

_____ .

An infected body cell will display **(13)** _____ of an invader

on its surface. These are substances that trigger an immune response.

In an immune response, B cells divide and develop into

(14) _____ _____ , which release

special defensive proteins into the blood. These special proteins are called

(15) _____ .

In the space provided, write the letter of the description that best matches the term or phrase.

_____16. Koch's postulates

_____ 17. immunity

_____18. vaccination

_____19. vaccine

_____20. antigen shifting

_____21. autoimmune disease

_____22. AIDS

_____23. HIV

_____24. allergy

_____25. CD4

a. body's inappropriate response to a normally harmless antigen

b. when the body launches an immune response against its own cells

c. a medical procedure used to produce immunity

d. the virus that causes AIDS

e. a guide for identifying specific pathogens

f. resistance to a particular disease

g. a solution that contains a dead or modified pathogen that can no longer cause disease

h. acquired immunodeficiency syndrome

i. when a pathogen produces a new antigen that the immune system does not recognize

j. receptor protein recognized by HIV

Name _____ Class _____ Date _____

Test Prep Pretest

In the space provided, write the letter of the term or phrase that best completes each statement or best answers each question.

_____ 1. White blood cells that kill bacteria by engulfing them and then releasing chemicals that kill both the bacteria and themselves are
    a. macrophages.
    b. neutrophils.
    c. natural killer cells.
    d. helper T cells.

_____ 2. The temperature response is helpful in fighting bacteria because
    a. higher temperatures promote the activation of cellular proteins.
    b. lower temperatures promote the activation of cellular proteins.
    c. disease-causing bacteria do not grow well at high temperatures.
    d. disease-causing bacteria do not grow well at low temperatures.

_____ 3. The four main types of cells involved in the immune response are
    a. macrophages, cytotoxic T cells, helper T cells, and B cells.
    b. macrophages, red blood cells, helper T cells, and neutrophils.
    c. macrophages, red blood cells, helper T cells, and natural killer cells.
    d. red blood cells, cytotoxic T cells, helper T cells, and B cells.

Questions 4–7 refer to the figure at right, which shows an immune response.

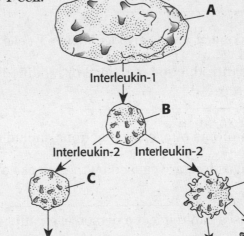

_____ 4. The cell labeled *A* is a
    a. macrophage. **c.** cytotoxic T cell.
    b. helper T cell. **d.** B cell.

_____ 5. The cell labeled *B* is a
    a. plasma cell.
    b. cytotoxic T cell.
    c. helper T cell.
    d. B cell.

_____ 6. The cell labeled *C* is a
    a. cytotoxic T cell.
    b. macrophage.
    c. plasma cell.
    d. memory cell.

_____ 7. The cells produced by the cell labeled *D*
    a. release antibodies.
    b. kill virus-infected cells.
    c. engulf viruses.
    d. secrete interleukin-2.

_____ **8.** In an autoimmune disease,
     a. a pathogen is immune to antigens.
     b. a pathogen circulates in the blood.
     c. the body attacks its own cells.
     d. the immune system collapses.

_____ **9.** Which of the following is NOT a way that HIV can be transmitted?
     a. sexual intercourse with an infected person
     b. injecting intravenous drugs with hypodermic needles contaminated with HIV-infected white blood cells
     c. blood transfusions in areas where tests for HIV are unavailable
     d. insect bites

Complete each statement by writing the correct term or phrase in the space provided.

10. Cells lining the bronchi and bronchioles in the respiratory tract secrete a layer of

_____ that traps pathogens before they can enter the lungs.

11. A chemical defense called the _____

_____ consists of about 20 different proteins that

circulate in the blood.

12. Helper T cells activate _____ T cells and

_____ cells.

13. To combat a viral invader, helper T cells release the protein _____ .

14. The introduction of a dead or modified pathogen into the body is

_____ .

15. Symptoms of allergic reactions, including swelling, itchy eyes, and nasal

congestion, are caused by the release of _____ .

16. Because of _____ _____ , influenza
viruses can reinfect a person even after memory cells have produced immunity.

17. An enzyme that prevents viruses from making proteins and RNA is the result

of a nonspecific defense called _____ .

18. Some cells of the immune system have receptor proteins that bind to specific

_____ .

Test Prep Pretest *continued*

Read each question, and write your answer in the space provided.

19. List Koch's postulates. How do biologists use Koch's postulates?

_____

_____

_____

_____

_____

_____

20. How can people decrease their exposure to pathogens?

_____

_____

21. What causes the pus that accompanies some infections?

_____

_____

22. Name three kinds of white blood cells involved in nonspecific defenses. Where are they found, and how does each type attack pathogens?

_____

_____

_____

_____

_____

23. How does a person become immune to a pathogen?

_____

_____

_____

_____

_____

_____

Test Prep Pretest *continued*

24. Name three autoimmune diseases and describe their symptoms.

_____

_____

_____

_____

_____

_____

_____

25. Describe the connection between HIV infection and a weakened immune system.

_____

_____

_____

_____

_____

Name _____ Class _____ Date _____

Vocabulary Review

In the space provided, write the letter of the description that best matches the term or phrase.

_____ 1. neuron

_____ 2. dendrite

_____ 3. axon

_____ 4. nerve

_____ 5. membrane potential

_____ 6. resting potential

_____ 7. action potential

_____ 8. synapse

_____ 9. neurotransmitter

a. the difference in electrical charge across a cell membrane

b. part of a neuron that conducts nerve impulses

c. the membrane potential of a neuron at rest

d. nerve cell; transmits information throughout the body

e. bundle of axons

f. part of a neuron that receives information from other neurons

g. a junction at which a neuron meets another cell

h. a signal molecule that transmits nerve impulses across synapses

i. nerve impulse

Write the correct term from the list below in the space next to its definition.

brain	hypothalamus	reflex
brain stem	interneurons	sensory neuron
central nervous system	motor neuron	spinal cord
cerebellum	peripheral nervous system	thalamus
cerebrum		

_____ **10.** sends commands from the central nervous system to muscles and other organs

_____ **11.** site of capacity for learning, memory, perception, and intellectual function

_____ **12.** consists of the brain and spinal cord

_____ **13.** relays sensory information to the cerebral cortex

_____ **14.** dense cable of nervous tissue that runs through the vertebral column

_____ **15.** contains sensory neurons and motor neurons

| Vocabulary Review *continued*

_____ 16. carries information from sense organs to the central nervous system

_____ 17. the body's main processing center

_____ 18. helps regulate breathing, heart rate, and endocrine functions

_____ 19. link neurons to each other

_____ 20. collection of structures leading down to the spinal cord

_____ 21. regulates balance, posture, and movement

_____ 22. a sudden, involuntary contraction of muscles in response to a stimulus

In the space provided, write the letter of the description that best matches the term or phrase.

_____ 23. sensory receptor

_____ 24. retina

_____ 25. rod

_____ 26. cone

_____ 27. optic nerve

_____ 28. cochlea

_____ 29. semicircular canal

a. the lining of photoreceptors and neurons in the eye

b. aids in hearing

c. type of photoreceptor that responds best to dim light

d. runs from the back of each eye to the brain

e. helps maintain equilibrium

f. a specialized neuron that detects sensory stimuli

g. type of photoreceptor that enables color vision

Complete each statement by writing the correct term or phrase in the space provided.

30. The need for increasing amounts of a drug to achieve the desired sensation

is called _____ .

31. A drug that generally decreases the activity of the central nervous system is

called a(n) _____ .

32. A drug that generally increases the activity of the central nervous system is

called a(n) _____ .

Vocabulary Review *continued*

33. Drugs that alter the functioning of the central nervous system are known as

_____ _____ .

34. A set of emotional and physical symptoms caused by removing a drug from

the body of a drug addict is _____ .

35. A physiological response caused by use of a drug that alters the normal

functioning of neurons and synapses is _____ .

Test Prep Pretest

In the space provided, write the letter of the term or phrase that best completes each statement or best answers each question.

_____ 1. During a knee-jerk reflex, the nerve impulse is received by the
   a. brain.
   b. spinal cord.
   c. spinal cord and then the brain.
   d. thalamus.

Questions 2–4 refer to the figure below, which shows the structure of a typical neuron.

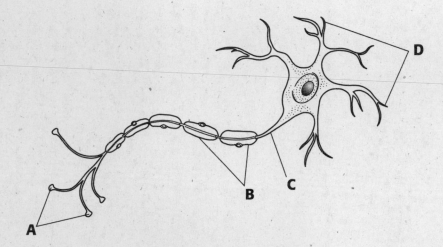

_____ 2. What occurs when an action potential reaches the structures labeled *A*?
   a. Neurotransmitters are released.
   b. Myelin sheaths are activated.
   c. Cell bodies receive messages.
   d. None of the above

_____ 3. The structures labeled *B* are
   a. axon terminals.   **c.** dendrites.
   b. nodes of Ranvier.   **d.** myelin sheaths.

_____ 4. The structures labeled *D* are
   a. dendrites.   **c.** axon terminals.
   b. axons.   **d.** nodes of Ranvier.

Test Prep Pretest *continued*

_____ 5. Light entering the eye stimulates
    a. hair cells in the retina.
    b. the optic nerve.
    c. rods and cones in the retina.
    d. mechanoreceptors.

_____ 6. When cocaine interferes with reuptake receptors on a presynaptic neuron, the
    a. postsynaptic cell is overstimulated.
    b. number of neurotransmitter receptors decreases.
    c. excess neurotransmitters remain in the synaptic cleft.
    d. All of the above

_____ 7. Drug use that alters normal functioning of neurons and synapses results in
    a. addiction.
    b. withdrawal.
    c. tolerance.
    d. None of the above

Questions 8–11 refer to the figure at right.

_____ 8. The structures labeled *A*, *B*, and *C* regulate
    a. heart rate and sleep.
    b. body temperature.
    c. breathing rate.
    d. All of the above

_____ 9. The structure labeled *D* is involved in
    a. balance and posture.
    b. maintaining homeostasis.
    c. learning, memory, and perception.
    d. spinal reflexes.

_____ 10. The structure labeled *E* is the
    a. thalamus.
    b. corpus callosum.
    c. brain stem.
    d. cerebrum.

_____ 11. The structure labeled *F* is the
    a. thalamus.
    b. hypothalamus.
    c. cerebellum.
    d. cerebral cortex.

Complete each statement by writing the correct term or phrase in the space provided.

12. The _____ _____ of a neuron is negative because there are more positively charged ions outside the cell than inside the cell.

13. A(n) _____ _____ is a local reversal of polarity inside a neuron.

14. During synaptic transmission, a presynaptic neuron releases a(n)

_____ into the synaptic _____ .

15. At a synapse, a neurotransmitter may _____ or

_____ the activity of the postsynaptic cell it binds to.

16. After a nerve impulse has passed, _____ ions flow out

of the axon, and the membrane potential becomes _____
again.

17. In the spinal cord, cell bodies of neurons make up the

_____ matter, while axons make up the

_____ matter.

18. The _____ nervous system contains neurons that connect the brain and the spinal cord to the rest of the body.

19. The coiled inner ear structure that converts sound waves to nerve impulses is

called the _____ .

20. Pain receptors are located on all tissues and organs except the

_____ .

21. Auditory information is processed in the _____

_____ of the brain.

22. Drugs that alter the functioning of the central nervous system and are often

addictive are called _____ _____ .

23. A(n) _____ is a substance that decreases the activity of the central nervous system.

Read each question, and write your answer in the space provided.

24. Distinguish between the somatic nervous system and the autonomic nervous system.

_____

_____

_____

_____

_____

_____

25. List the four basic types of chemicals that taste buds can detect.

_____

_____

Skills Worksheet

Vocabulary Review

In the space provided, write the letter of the description that best matches the term or phrase.

_____ 1. hormone

_____ 2. endocrine glands

_____ 3. target cell

_____ 4. amino-acid-based hormones

_____ 5. steroid hormones

_____ 6. second messenger

_____ 7. negative feedback

_____ 8. hypothalamus

_____ 9. pituitary gland

_____ 10. adrenal glands

_____ 11. epinephrine

_____ 12. norepinephrine

_____ 13. insulin

_____ 14. glucagon

_____ 15. diabetes mellitus

a. structure of the brain that coordinates the activities of the nervous and endocrine systems

b. a hormone that lowers blood glucose levels

c. condition in which cells are unable to obtain glucose from the blood

d. a specific cell on which a hormone acts

e. a change in one direction stimulates the control mechanism to counteract further change in the same direction

f. substances that are secreted by cells and that act to regulate the activity of other cells

g. a molecule that passes a chemical message from the first messenger to the cell

h. a hormone that causes liver cells to release glucose

i. ductless organs that secrete hormones directly into either the bloodstream or the fluid around cells

j. one of two hormones released in time of stress; formerly called adrenaline

k. lipid hormones the body makes from cholesterol

l. secretes many hormones, including some that control endocrine glands elsewhere in the body

m. mostly water-soluble hormones

n. endocrine organs located above each kidney

o. one of two hormones released in time of stress; formerly called noradrenaline

Skills Worksheet

Test Prep Pretest

In the space provided, write the letter of the term or phrase that best completes each statement or best answers each question.

_____ 1. Which of the following is NOT a characteristic of the endocrine system?
   a. Its chemical messengers are neurotransmitters.
   b. It coordinates all of the body's sources of hormones.
   c. Endocrine cells can release hormones directly into the bloodstream.
   d. Its chemical messengers bind to receptors.

_____ 2. Which of the following is a function of hormones?
   a. regulating growth
   b. maintaining homeostasis
   c. reacting to stimuli
   d. All of the above

_____ 3. A hormone acts only on its target cell by
   a. stimulating a nerve cell.
   b. recognizing a receptor protein on or in the target cell.
   c. binding to a nerve cell.
   d. activating an enzyme in the blood.

_____ 4. The testes produce
   a. estrogen.
   b. progesterone.
   c. testosterone.
   d. oxytocin.

_____ 5. Epinephrine and norepinephrine are released in response to
   a. falling levels of calcium in the blood.
   b. rising levels of calcium in the blood.
   c. stress.
   d. rising levels of glucose in the blood.

_____ 6. Aldosterone helps to
   a. excrete sodium ions in the urine.
   b. decrease the volume of blood.
   c. decrease blood pressure.
   d. reabsorb sodium ions from fluids removed by the kidneys.

Complete each statement by writing the correct term or phrase in the space provided.

7. Ductless organs that produce hormones are called _____

_____.

8. Hormones that are fat soluble are _____ hormones.

9. A group of neuropeptides that are thought to regulate emotions and influence

pain are _____ .

10. The release of _____ from the posterior pituitary
stimulates uterine contractions and milk secretion.

11. When a steroid hormone binds to a receptor protein in a target cell's

cytoplasm, a(n) _____-_____
complex is produced.

12. In a(n) _____ _____ mechanism,
high levels of a hormone inhibit the output of more hormone.

13. High levels of the adrenal cortex hormone, called _____ ,
suppress the immune system.

14. The _____ and the _____ gland
together serve as a major control center for the rest of the endocrine system.

15. The thyroid gland releases _____ in response to high
blood calcium levels.

16. Hormones that regulate the body's metabolic rate and promote normal growth

of the brain, bones, and muscles are _____ hormones.

17. The _____ _____ secretes the
hormone melatonin in response to darkness.

Read each question, and write your answer in the space provided.

18. Describe the role of second messengers in relaying a hormone's message.

_____

_____

_____

_____

_____

| Test Prep Pretest *continued*

19. What two basic types of hormones does the hypothalamus send to the anterior pituitary, and what are their functions?

_____

_____

_____

_____

20. Explain how the pancreatic hormones insulin and glucagon regulate blood glucose levels.

_____

_____

_____

_____

_____

_____

Vocabulary Review

Write the correct term from the list below in the space next to its definition.

bulbourethral glands	prostate gland	seminiferous tubules
epididymis	semen	testes
penis	seminal vesicles	vas deferens

_____ **1.** produce a sugar-rich fluid that sperm use for energy

_____ **2.** long tube that connects the epididymis to the urethra

_____ **3.** the gamete-producing organs of the male reproductive system

_____ **4.** secretes an alkaline fluid that neutralizes the acids in the female reproductive system

_____ **5.** a mixture of exocrine secretions and sperm

_____ **6.** secrete an alkaline fluid that neutralizes traces of acidic urine in the male urethra

_____ **7.** site within testes where sperm are produced

_____ **8.** the male organ that deposits sperm in the female reproductive system during sexual intercourse

_____ **9.** site where sperm cells mature

In the space provided, write the letter of the description that best matches the term or phrase.

_____ **10.** gestation

_____ **11.** placenta

_____ **12.** cleavage

_____ **13.** fetus

_____ **14.** embryo

_____ **15.** blastocyst

_____ **16.** implantation

_____ **17.** pregnancy

a. a hollow ball of zygotic cells

b. period of development; pregnancy

c. a series of internal divisions that the zygote undergoes in the first week after fertilization

d. a developing human during the first 8 weeks after fertilization

e. burrowing of the blastocyst into the lining of the uterus

f. a developing human from the eighth week of pregnancy until birth

g. a structure through which the mother nourishes the fetus

h. divided into three trimesters

Vocabulary Review *continued*

Complete each statement by writing the correct term or phrase in the space provided.

18. The release of an ovum is called _____ .

19. The _____ are the gamete-producing organs of the female reproductive system.

20. The _____ _____ is the series of hormone-induced changes involved in the preparation and release of an ovum.

21. A mature egg cell is called a(n) _____ .

22. A(n) _____ _____ is a mass of follicular cells that secretes estrogen and progesterone.

23. A(n) _____ is a cluster of cells that surrounds an immature egg cell and provides the egg with nutrients.

24. The _____ is the hollow, muscular organ in which development occurs.

25. The shedding of the lining of the uterus is called _____ .

26. The _____ is the muscular tube that leads from the outside of a female's body to the uterus.

27. Each _____ _____ is a passageway through which an ovum moves from an ovary toward the uterus.

28. The series of hormone-induced changes that prepare the uterus for a possible pregnancy each month is called the _____

_____ .

29. A bacterial STD that causes painful urination and a discharge of pus from the

penis in males is _____ . In females, it sometimes causes a vaginal discharge.

30. A serious bacterial STD that usually begins with a small, painless ulcer called

a chancre 2–3 weeks after infection is _____ .

31. The symptoms of _____ , a bacterial STD, are similar to those of a mild case of gonorrhea and can cause scar tissue in infected fallopian tubes, leading to infertility.

32. One of the most common causes of infertility in women is

_____ _____ _____ ,

which is a severe inflammation of the uterus, ovaries, fallopian tubes, or
abdominal cavity that results from an untreated bacterial STD.

33. A viral STD that includes periodic outbreaks of painful blisters in the genital

region, flulike aches, and fever is _____

_____ .

Test Prep Pretest

In the space provided, write the letter of the term or phrase that best completes each statement or best answers each question.

_____ 1. Sperm cells are produced by meiosis in the
   a. epididymis.
   b. vas deferens.
   c. seminiferous tubules.
   d. scrotum.

_____ 2. The gamete-producing organs of the female reproductive system are the
   a. corpus luteum.
   b. fallopian tubes.
   c. ovaries.
   d. seminiferous tubules.

_____ 3. When the zygote reaches the uterus, it is a hollow ball of cells called a(n)
   a. embryo.   **c.** egg.
   b. blastocyst.   **d.** fetus.

_____ 4. It is especially important that pregnant women abstain from
   a. vitamins prescribed by a doctor.
   b. moderate exercise.
   c. alcohol.
   d. vegetables such as cauliflower and broccoli.

_____ 5. Viral STDs
   a. can be treated and cured successfully using antibiotics.
   b. cannot be treated and cured successfully using antibiotics.
   c. cannot cause death if untreated.
   d. cannot be passed to a fetus.

Complete each statement by writing the correct term or phrase in the space provided.

6. A fatal disease caused by the human immunodeficiency virus (HIV) is

   _____ .

7. One of the most common causes of infertility in women, a condition linked to

   bacterial STDs, is _____ _____

   _____ .

Test Prep Pretest *continued*

Questions 8 and 9 refer to the figure below, which shows a mature sperm cell.

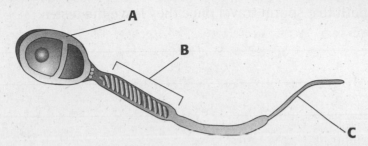

Complete each statement by writing the correct term or phrase in the space provided.

8. The structure labeled *A*, called the _____ , contains enzymes that help the sperm penetrate an ovum.

9. The energy that sperm need for movement is supplied by ATP produced in the

_____ , labeled *B*. This energy powers the whiplike

movements of the _____ , labeled *C*.

10. The testes are located outside the body cavity in an external skin sac called

the _____ .

11. _____ and _____ occurs before inplantation of the blastocyst.

12. The _____ _____ begins when the anterior pituitary releases follicle-stimulating hormone and luteinizing hormone into the bloodstream.

13. When a follicle bursts, the mature egg cell is released in a process called

_____ .

14. During _____ , the lining of the uterus is shed, blood vessels are broken, and bleeding results.

15. The embryonic membrane called the _____ encloses the embryo.

16. Most _____ STDs can be treated and cured using antibiotics.

17. By the end of the _____ trimester, a fetus is able to exist outside the mother's body.

Test Prep Pretest *continued*

Read each question, and write your answer in the space provided.

18. Trace the path that sperm travel once they leave the testes.

_____

_____

_____

_____

_____

19. Describe the events that occur early in the first trimester of pregnancy.

_____

_____

_____

_____

Question 20 refers to the figure at right, which shows the female reproductive system.

20. Identify the structures labeled *A–D*, and describe the functions of these structures.

_____

_____

_____

_____

_____

_____

_____

_____

_____

_____

_____